Institute of Criminology, University of Cambridge

CAMBRIDGE STUDIES IN CRIMINOLOGY

EDITED BY

L. RADZINOWICZ, LL.D.

VOLUME XV

JUDICIAL ATTITUDES
IN SENTENCING

JUDICIAL ATTITUDES IN SENTENCING

A Study of the Factors
underlying the Sentencing Practice of the
Criminal Court of Philadelphia

BY

EDWARD GREEN, Ph.D.

GREENWOOD PRESS, PUBLISHERS
WESTPORT, CONNECTICUT

Library of Congress Cataloging in Publication Data

Green, Edward, 1920-
  Judicial attitudes in sentencing.

    Reprint of the ed. published by Macmillan, London,
  and St. Martin's Press, New York, which was issued as
  v. 15 of Cambridge studies in criminology.
    Originally presented as the author's thesis,
  University of Pennsylvania, 1959, under title: An
  analysis of sentencing practices of criminal court
  judges in Philadelphia.
    Bibliography: p.
    Includes index.
    1. Sentences (Criminal procedure)--Philadelphia.
  2. Psychology, Forensic. I. Title. II. Series:
  Cambridge studies in criminology ; v. 15.
  KFX2137.G7 1974   345'.74811'077   74-17589
  ISBN 0-8371-7834-7

Originally published in 1961 by Macmillan & Co. Ltd., London
and St. Martin's Press, New York

Reprinted with the permission of St. Martin's Press, Inc.

Reprinted in 1974 by Greenwood Press,
a division of Williamhouse-Regency Inc.

Library of Congress Catalog Card Number 74-17589

ISBN 0-8371-7834-7

Printed in the United States of America

CONTENTS

ACKNOWLEDGEMENTS

THE AUTHOR gratefully acknowledges the many kindnesses of those who contributed to the completion and publication of this research, particularly the assistance of the following. Judge Joseph Sloane of the Philadelphia Court of Quarter Sessions was a valuable consultant and ally. The staff of the Quarter Sessions Court was unfailingly helpful and courteous. Former Police Commissioner Thomas J. Gibbons of the City of Philadelphia graciously granted access to the police records. The wholehearted cooperation of the staff in the records section of the police department facilitated immeasurably the collection of the data. I am indebted to Professor Thorsten Sellin of the University of Pennsylvania for his mentorship and his interest which gave rise to the publication of the research, and to Professor Leon Radzinowicz for his guidance in the preparation of the manuscript for publication.

E. GREEN

PREFACE

BY THE DIRECTOR OF THE INSTITUTE

A SALIENT feature of criminal law in the English-speaking countries is the exceptionally wide discretionary power vested in the courts. This reflects both a native empiricism and a native confidence that such power will not be abused. The range of discretion is very wide: only capital crimes carry a fixed sentence, whilst others may involve anything from life imprisonment to discharge.

Sentencing practice is an aspect of criminal justice which will continue to arouse wide interest amongst administrators, criminologists and, indeed, the courts themselves. How do they reconcile the two fundamental objects of securing equality in punishment and treatment and of adapting them to the personality of the offender and the nature of the offence? Whilst recognising that disparities in sentencing are to a large extent inevitable, it is important to know how wide they are, and also what factors guide the courts in the choice of sanctions.

"Sentencing", states the Inter-departmental Committee on the Business of the Criminal Courts, "used to be a comparatively simple matter. The primary object was to fix a sentence proportionate to the offender's culpability, and the system has been loosely described as the 'tariff system'.... In many cases, particularly those appearing at the superior courts, the court can still do little more than punish the offender for what he has done, and in every sentence the offender's culpability has to be taken into account. But in a considerable and growing number of cases the 'tariff system' can no longer be relied on to fit all the considerations in the court's mind. The need to deter or reform the offender, the need to protect society, and the need to deter potential offenders may in a particular case be conflicting considerations. These objectives have an importance of their own and have a separate effect on the decision of the court." Sentencing has now become a much more complex task and is, in a sense, "... an emergent branch of the law". And yet there is hardly a subject in

vii

the entire field of criminal justice which has been less explored and upon which we still know so little.

The value of Professor Green's monograph lies in the fact that, eschewing wide generalisations, he has made an objective and concrete study of the working of a particular court, attempting to assess the degrees of uniformity and disparity in its sentences, their range, and the criteria by which they are decided. He has discharged this task in an original and stimulating way. Though the basis of his enquiry was the practice of the court at Philadelphia, his study has much wider significance, both in its methods and its conclusions, and will undoubtedly be read with great interest in this country as well as in his own.

L.R.

INSTITUTE OF CRIMINOLOGY
UNIVERSITY OF CAMBRIDGE
June, 1961

I

INTRODUCTION

No aspect of the administration of criminal justice has aroused as much concern among jurists and criminologists as the sentencing of convicted offenders. The immense responsibility of the sentencing judge to both the community and the defendant; the dilemmas posed by the conflicting claims of modern rehabilitative philosophy, legal tradition, and public opinion which the conscientious judge must often face alone; and the problem of inequalities in sentencing — these are the focal points of discussion in the extensive body of critical exposition on the sentencing problem. The factual basis of the opinions expressed upon these questions is usually either conjectural or rooted in the findings of research studies whose designs reveal an indifference toward the legal complexities of the sentencing process. Accordingly, the present study will attempt to supply a factual and theoretical perspective on the sentencing process by investigating more extensively than hitherto has been done the factors which underlie variation in the gravity of the penalties meted out to convicted offenders.

THE PROBLEM

The period since the beginning of the twentieth century has witnessed a continuing tendency in the United States toward widening the discretion of the sentencing judge. Legal innovations, notably the indeterminate sentence and probation, have infused greater flexibility into the administration of criminal justice at the expense of precision and certainty in the law. The judge in sentencing is bound within broad limits by the traditional view of crime and criminals embodied in the penal statutes. These provide for penalties graded according to the enormity of the offence. He is also under strong pressure to bring his sentencing practices into line with rehabilitative goals which emphasize the treatment of the offender rather than punishment. The vain attempt to accommodate these seemingly inconsistent objectives has resulted in a lack of specific guides for sentencing, a condition which has stimulated a lively controversy regarding basic issues of penal philosophy and the administration of criminal justice.

The debate on the sentencing problem has focused upon three closely related issues: the objectives of punishment, the criteria for sentencing, and the consistency of sentencing.

The objectives of punishment

The design of the penal codes currently in force in the various states of the United States was inspired by the classical school of criminal jurisprudence stemming from the Enlightenment of the eighteenth century. Conceived as a protest against the excesses of physical cruelty wreaked upon convicted criminals in the name of expiation or retribution, the classical jurisprudence repudiated vengeance as a proper aim of criminal justice and affirmed that the sole justification of punishment is the deterrence of crime. This objective was to be accomplished by striking a proportion between the evil of the crime and its penalty such that the pain of the punishment would outweigh the pleasure to be had from the offence. This theme was elaborated in minute detail by the architects of the classical theory of punishment, among them Jeremy Bentham, whose rules of "moral arithmetic" attempted to impart to the criminal law the quality of a rational science. Nevertheless, Bentham recognized that the punishment for the same offence might properly vary according to circumstances.[1]

The major opposition to the classical theory of punishment stems from the positive school of criminology, a product of nineteenth-century social science. The positivists, rejecting the hedonistic psychology of the classicists, postulate that the causes of criminal behaviour lie in antecedents which can be studied by scientific methods and urge that the knowledge thereby acquired should be the basis of programmes for the scientific control of crime. They attack the objectives of punishment — whether expiation, retribution, or deterrence — on the ground that such ends are either unworthy of a civilized society or of limited efficacy. They call for a programme of individualized treatment designed to rehabilitate the offender or, if he is incorrigible, to isolate him indefinitely. Some positivists doubt that the judge's formal training qualifies

[1] Jeremy Bentham, *The Theory of Legislation*, ed. C. R. Ogden (New York: Harcourt, Brace and Co., 1931), p. 325.

him to arrive at a just sentence; they would limit the role of the judge to refereeing the trial and transfer the sentencing function to a panel of experts trained in the sciences of human behaviour. A more moderate proposal recommends the establishment of sentencing boards to act merely in an advisory capacity to the judge.

The present-day condition of juridical thought in the United States shows some effects of the vigorous attack of the positivists. With the acceptance of the view that environmental pressures or disordered states of mind might impede the offender's ability to calculate rationally the risks of pleasure and pain involved in criminal conduct, the judiciary came to recognize varying degrees of guilt for the same offence. This modified view, or neo-classical school, is the foundation of the present-day system of Anglo-American criminal jurisprudence. Although acknowledging the values of reform and rehabilitation, it places the protection of society above them and continues to assert the deterrent value of punishment to achieve that end. This is the position taken by the framers of the American Law Institute's *Model Penal Code* and supported by a probably decisive majority of the American judiciary. In this view, the objective sought by the judge need not be the same in all cases. As Judge William J. Campbell, an American federal court judge, has pointed out, where rehabilitation is the prime concern, the treatment should be tailored to the individual; in extreme cases of antisocial offenders, prolonged confinement assures the protection of society. Where, however, the law violation is a matter of principle, such as draft violation, and where ". . . there is no question of rehabilitation . . . they (offenders) must be sentenced as examples; otherwise, human nature being what it is, we would most assuredly be faced with great numbers of less stable citizens seeking ways and means to avoid military service".[1] Even retribution is allowed as an objective of sentencing where the crime is ". . . revolting and incomprehensible to the group".[2]

The criteria for sentencing

The controversy over the criteria employed in sentencing has produced the same ideological alignment as the debate on the

---

[1] Judge William J. Campbell, "Developing Systematic Sentencing Procedures," *Federal Probation*, XVIII (September 1954) pp. 3–9.

[2] *Ibid.*, p. 6.

goals of justice. Nevertheless, the partisans on both sides decry the lack of uniform standards or the intrusion of irrelevant criteria in the administration of criminal justice. For purposes of this review, the criteria for sentencing are assigned to three categories: statutory factors, discretionary factors, and legally irrelevant factors.

Statutory factors. The first consists of the formal set of standards provided by the penal code for the determination of the relative gravity of crimes and laws providing additional penalties for recidivists.

Certain common law distinctions retained in statutory law — felonies and misdemeanours, grand larceny and petit larceny — roughly differentiate between offences of greater and lesser degree. The penal codes contain an elaborate classification of crimes with their corresponding penalties finely graded according to the seriousness of the crime. We find, however, that within a given jurisdiction at a given time the gradation of the crimes is not systematically derived in accordance with a logically consistent scheme of values; rather it is an historical product reflecting the social exigencies of the various times in which the statutes were enacted. In the penal code of Pennsylvania, for example, the offence of breaking into a store and stealing a carton of cigarettes (burglary) carries potentially as high a penalty (imprisonment for 20 years) as a wilful act of homicide (second degree murder). Sexual intercourse with a willing female under sixteen years of age (statutory rape), even though she be of mature appearance, entails the risk of imprisonment for five times as long a term (15 years) as a physical assault with a deadly weapon (aggravated assault and battery) upon the same female. Assault with intent to rob carries a higher maximum penalty (imprisonment for 10 years) than assault with intent to kill (imprisonment for 7 years), presumably a worse fate.

The law requires that the punishment fit the crime but the standards of measurement are vague. Under the indeterminate sentencing procedures in force in most state jurisdictions of the United States, the statutes do not stipulate specific penalties for the various offences but rather indicate the limits of the range from which the judge may select the appropriate sentence. In Pennsylvania, the penal statutes fix only the upper limit of the term of a prison sentence or the amount of a fine which may be imposed for particular crimes. Thus the statutory scale of penalties consists not of a series of points on a continuum of sanctions but rather of a series of overlapping ranges. Within these statutory limitations, the judge theoretically may exercise a vast discretion in adjusting the magnitude of the type of sentence he decides upon — imprisonment, probation, fine, or suspended sentence — to accord with his penal philosophy.

Discretionary criteria. The standards available to the judge for determining the penalty in a given case emanate from the ethical and moral order of which the law is a part but which the law can only imperfectly mirror, particularly in a rapidly changing society with a diversity of regional and local cultural traditions. They pertain to the circumstances of the criminal act, the characteristics of the offender, and the attitudes and sentiments of the community toward certain types of crimes or criminals. With respect to the first and second categories, Judge Theodore Levin specifies the following questions which the judge should consider in the determination of a sentence.[1]

Was the crime against person or property? If the former, did it endanger the life of the victim or leave permanent effects upon his general welfare? Was it premeditated or was it the result of an impulse arising from a fit of passion? Does the background of the offender reveal a pattern of transgressions of the law? Are the circumstances such as to indicate that there was no full appreciation of the nature and significance of the behaviour which constituted the offence? Are the offender's emotional and mental characteristics, his family ties, and his business interests such as to offer encouragement and hope for his reformation, or is he likely again to collide with the rules of living established by society? Does the individual before the court, having regard to the public interests, require punishment greater than the impact upon him of the conviction itself? Is he an individual upon whom a term of imprisonment may reasonably be expected to have a corrective effect? Will irreparable damage result to the family group if he is removed from it? Is there any indication that a severe sentence will act as a deterrent upon others who might be prone to commit crime?

Commenting on the community factor, the publication of the National Probation and Parole Association, *Guides to Sentencing* advises the judge not to be dominated by community sentiment where it militates against judicial conscience but to strive, never-

[1] Judge Theodore Levin, "Sentencing the Criminal Offender," *Federal Probation*, XIII (March 1949), pp. 3–4. See also Judge Alexander Holtzoff, "The Judicial Process as Applied to Sentencing in Criminal Cases," *Federal Probation*, XIV (June 1950), pp. 52–6; and Judge William J. Campbell, *op. cit.*

theless, to render decisions that do not outrage the public sensibility.[1] Morris Cohen in presenting his philosophy of law propounds a similar view:[2]

> It is also well to note the superior wisdom of the law (as against abstract moralists) in recognizing the claim of custom or the *status quo* as such. The latter create expectations and to shock or defeat them is to effect an evil justified only if a greater evil can thereby be avoided.

The principles governing the application of the statutory and discretionary criteria are deeply imbedded in the Anglo-American legal tradition. The criminal law rests upon the doctrine that human conduct is self-determined; that man has the capacity to distinguish between right and wrong and to choose freely among alternative course of conduct. Nevertheless, it recognizes certain exceptions to this rule: children under the age at which the law presumes them to be capable of harbouring a criminal intent and adults whose state of mind at the time of the crime fails to meet certain tests of rational capacity.

Probably a decided majority of academic criminologists oppose the doctrine that the human actor is a free moral agent. Even those who do not reject it philosophically organize their research or interpretations in terms of the assumption that criminal behaviour, like non-criminal behaviour, is a function of biologic, psychologic, psychiatric, cultural, and sociologic factors. They regard the penal codes with their gradation of crimes and punishments and the guilt determining aspect of the criminal trial procedure as prescientific legalism.

Legally irrelevant criteria. These include political or journalistic pressures, public hysteria, prejudice against minority groups, and the personality of the sentencing judge — factors that are discordant with the proper goals of criminal justice. Numerous claims are made by jurists and criminologists that these elements exert an enormous influence on the judge's sentences. Most of the opinions on this subject converge toward the view that the state of the judge's humour, his digestion, his unconscious fears and desires — in short, the caprices of "judicial temperament" — determine the penalties imposed on criminal offenders.

---

[1] Advisory Council of Judges of the National Probation and Parole Association, *Guides to Sentencing* (New York: Carnegie Press, 1957), pp. 45 ff.

[2] Morris R. Cohen, *Reason and Law* (Glencoe, Illinois: The Free Press, 1950), p. 7.

A version of this view cast in terms of psychoanalytic theory[1] asserts that judges' opinions, on close analysis, turn out to be intellectualizations and rationalizations of unconscious impulses; fear and shame are unconsciously projected into opinions, and unconscious defences are marshalled to preclude suspicion of disapproved behaviour from resting upon the judge. Henry Weihofen,[2] in writing of the resistance in criminal law circles to mental disorder as a criminal defence, comments in a similar vein:

> It is not only criminals who are motivated by irrational impulsions, the same is true of lawyers and judges . . . and it is especially true on such a subject as the punishment of criminals.

Sociological variants of this theme stated in terms of *class* or *culture conflict* are adduced in studies indicating inequality in the sentencing of defendants with minority-group status.[3]

The consistency of sentencing

The severest criticism of sentencing practices in American courts is directed at the disparities in sentences for cases of equivalent gravity. The compilers of a bibliography on disparities in sentencing[4] summarize the general view of this problem as follows:

> While in theory the sentences meted out to two offenders convicted of the identical crime may and should differ depending upon such extrinsic factors as psychiatric and social worker reports, past criminal records, and estimates of future potentialities, there has been for years widespread fear that marked variances in treatment are the result of nothing more than the predilections of individual judges. Various studies have been undertaken to substantiate this thesis and have generally concluded that illogical disparities in sentencing and the utilization of parole facilities do exist.

A few observers, however, regard the lack of uniformity in sentences as the inevitable outcome of attempts at individualization. As one Pennsylvania jurist puts it: "With the admission that unequal periods of confinement must necessarily follow the theory

---

[1] Theodore Schroeder, "The Psychologic Study of Judicial Opinions," *California Law Review*, VI (January 1918), pp. 89–113.

[2] Henry Weihofen, *The Urge to Punish* (New York: Farrar, Straus and Cudahy, 1956), p. 132. See also Franz Alexander and Hugo Staub, *The Criminal, the Judge, and the Public*, rev. ed. (Glencoe, Illinois: The Free Press, 1956), pp. 209–23.

[3] *Infra*, pp. 8–11.

[4] Institute of Judicial Administration, *Disparity in Sentencing of Convicted Offenders* (New York: April 1954).

of individualization, statistics on sentence differences have little value."[1]

To sum up the trend of present-day thought regarding the sentencing problem in the American courts, we refer to the general view of the administration of criminal justice expressed by the authors of criminology textbooks published in the United States. The opinions of these writers[2] range from moderate criticism to virtually blanket condemnation of the courts — their policies, their procedures, and even the calibre of the judiciary who staff them. The principal complaints are the lack of any well-defined philosophical orientation, the intrusion of prejudice and irrelevant factors into judical decisions, and the grossly disparate sentences for cases of equivalent gravity.

REVIEW OF RESEARCH STUDIES OF SENTENCING

Studies of the sentencing behaviour of criminal court judges are relatively few and, for reasons which will be elaborated, have limited application to the resolution of the issues treated above. All of them stress the theme of the non-rationality of the sentencing process. None of them includes a systematic analysis of the legal criteria for sentencing. We shall consider first the studies investigating the differential treatment of minority groups and then those studies dealing with the problem of disparities among judges in sentencing.

Thorsten Sellin has contributed two investigations of differences in sentences according to race. The earlier one[3] presents police statistics on the disposition of cases in the Recorders Court of Detroit, Michigan, which show that the judges impose harsher sentences upon Negro defendants than upon white defendants. The former receive a much smaller percentage of probations than the whites (7·2 : 12·2) and twice the percentage of prison sentences

---

[1] Burton R. Laub, "Sentencing and Release in Pennsylvania — A New Approach," *Temple Law Quarterly*, XXVII (Spring 1954), p. 435.

[2] Harry Elmer Barnes and Negley K. Teeters, *New Horizons in Criminology*, 2nd ed. (New York: Prentice-Hall, Inc., 1951), pp. 285–95; Mabel A. Elliot, *Crime in Modern Society* (New York: Harper & Bros., 1952); Arthur E. Wood and John B. Waite, *Crime and its Treatment* (New York: American Book Co., 1941); Ruth S. Cavan, *Criminology* (New York: Thos. Y. Crowell Co., 1955); Edwin H. Sutherland and Donald R. Cressey, *Principles of Criminology*, 5th ed. (Chicago: J. B. Lippincott Co., 1955); Robert G. Caldwell, *Criminology* (New York: The Ronald Press Co., 1956).

[3] Thorsten Sellin, "The Negro Criminal: A Statistical Note," *Annals of the American Academy of Political and Social Science*, CXL (November 1928), pp. 52–64.

(30·9: 15·5). Data on racial differences in recidivism or in the distribution of various types of crimes are not available in this study, but the author considers the possible, though not likely, influence of these factors in producing the differences in sentences.

The later study[1] based upon data for the United States is an investigation of differences among native-born whites, foreign-born whites, and Negroes in the length of prison sentences received for ten different offences. In the states employing definite sentences, the Negroes receive longer average sentences than the whites in only three out of ten offence categories; but in the states employing indeterminate sentences, Negroes receive longer minima for all offences except homicide and longer maxima for all offences except assault and burglary. Since the majority of the determinate sentences were imposed in Southern states and the vast majority of the indeterminate sentences were imposed in Northern states, Sellin infers that the greater leniency shown Negroes in the South reflects a paternalistic attitude toward the Negro which carries over from the period of slavery; whereas in the North, the Negro ". . . is not only a competitor in industry but an 'outsider' ".[2] Sellin concedes that differences in sentences may be due in part to the influence of such uninvestigated factors as recidivism and aggravated circumstances, but he attributes most of the variation to the "human equation in judicial administration".[3]

Roscoe Martin's study of the relationship between the social traits of the defendant and the outcome of the various procedural steps in the administration of criminal justice[4] is based upon a 10 per cent sample of the felony cases disposed of in the district courts of Texas in the year 1930. Martin found that the courts favour native Americans over Negroes, Mexicans, and "others" (European-born whites); defendants native to the county of trial over, in the order named, Texans not native to the county of trial, American-born non-Texans, and foreign-born persons; defendants engaged in trade over those in lower grade occupational categories (manufacturing, mechanical, domestic and personal services); defendants who are property owners over propertyless defendants; the taxpayer over the tax delinquent; married men over single men; the widowed over the divorced; defendants with children

---

[1] Thorsten Sellin, "Race Prejudice in the Administration of Justice," *American Journal of Sociology*, XLI (September 1935), pp. 212–17.

[2] *Ibid.*, p. 217.   [3] *Ibid.*

[4] Roscoe Martin, *The Defendant and Criminal Justice* (University of Texas Bulletin No. 3437: Bureau of Research in the Social Sciences, Study No. 9, 1 October 1934).

over those who are childless; and poll taxpayers over non-poll taxpayers. Variables having no effect upon the severity of the sentences are sex, age, amount of education, and the presence or absence of parents.

Martin, in arriving at his conclusions, does not, however, consider a part of his data[1] which shows that the differences in sentences noted above are accompanied by marked differences in the proportions of offences of varying gravity, the defendants in the lower status groups committing a greater proportion of crimes entailing more severe penalties. The Negro and Mexican groups, each, compared with the whites, commit proportionately more than twice as many crimes against the person including murder, assault to murder, robbery and rape ($23\cdot9\%$, 25% : $9\cdot9\%$). The percentage of these crimes is greater in the cases of defendants born abroad (who are nearly all Mexicans) than in the cases o defendants born in Texas ($21\cdot9\%$: 16%). Likewise, offenders engaged in trade commit these offences to a much lesser extent ($13\cdot4\%$) than those engaged in mechanical industries ($15\cdot7\%$), domestic service ($20\cdot1\%$), or personal service (40%). Thus it is very likely that the heavier penalties accorded to the minority groups primarily reflect the differences in the kind of crimes they commit rather than any judicial prejudice against them.

A more recent study by Edwin M. Lemert and Judy Rosberg[2] investigates differences in the penalties dealt out to Negro, Mexican, and white offenders in the Superior Court of Los Angeles County in the year 1938. The authors find that the whites receive considerably milder sentences than either the Negroes or the Mexicans. They regard these differences as a form of discrimination incident to the struggle for power among social classes.

The evidence, however, is of questionable sufficiency owing to inadequate experimental controls. A comparison of the three racial groups within five offence categories with respect to the proportion of probations granted shows clearly that the whites are favoured. However, no control for the degree of recidivism is imposed in making these comparisons. The seriousness of this omission is pointed up by the results of another experiment in the study which show that for the crime of rape with recidivism con-

[1] *Ibid.*, p. 43.
[2] Edwin M. Lemert and Judy Rosberg, "The Administration of Justice to Minority Groups in Los Angeles County," *University of California Publications in Culture and Society*, Vol. II, No. 1 (1948), pp. 1–28

trol, the Negroes and Mexicans receive as large a proportion of probations as do the whites, the differences in sentences being statistically non-significant.

Additional comparisons investigating the differences among the races in the distribution of penalties for particular crimes yield results indicative of minority-group prejudice. Yet, in the two instances where the investigators impose a rigorous control for variation in recidivism, the differences in penalties among the three races turn out to be statistically non-significant. One instance has already been mentioned, the comparison in cases of rape. Another is the comparison of the sentences meted out to unskilled labourers in each of the three racial groups for the crimes of auto theft and second degree burglary combined. In cases having no previous record, there are no statistically significant differences in sentences; in cases having a prior felony record, the whites received significantly lighter penalties. The control imposed in the latter experiment, "prior felony record", is insensitive to possible differences between whites and racial minorities in the *number* of prior felony convictions, a factor which is very likely to influence the judge's determination of the sentence.

The fact that in some of the comparisons, the differences in sentences between Negroes and Mexicans are as marked as those between whites and non-whites suggests that cultural differences among the racial groups in criminal behaviour patterns are in some measure responsible for the variations in the severity of the sentences. Obviously, it is necessary to explore this possibility before arriving at any firm conclusion concerning racial discrimination in sentencing.

Turning now to studies of individual differences in the sentencing practices of criminal court judges, we find a diversity of approaches. Some investigators take as their subject matter cases of petty violations adjudicated in inferior courts; others employ the data of cases in courts of criminal jurisdiction. Some compare the sentences of courts in different political subdivisions; others compare the sentences of judges rotating in the same court. One study compares the sentences of felons committed to a state penitentiary without regard to the sentencing judge.

One of the earliest studies is George Everson's comparison of the sentencing records of New York City magistrates for the year 1914.[1]

---

[1] George Everson, "The Human Element in Justice," *Journal of the American Institute of Criminal Law and Criminology*, X (May 1919), pp. 90–4.

One hundred and fifty-three thousand cases of summary violations of local ordinances: intoxication, disorderly conduct, etc. were disposed of by forty-two magistrates sitting in rotation in twenty-eight courts. The results of the study lead Everson to conclude that "justice is a very personal thing", that marked variations in sentencing are due to the individuality of the magistrate and reflect his temperament, personality, and education.[1]

This conclusion rests upon evidence consisting primarily of data on the disposition of cases of intoxication. No information on the cases other than the charge is given. The percentage of cases discharged by each of forty-one magistrates in 17,073 cases of intoxication ranges from as few as 0·2 per cent to as many as 78·9 per cent. Close inspection of the data reveals, however, that thirty-four of the magistrates who disposed of 71 per cent of the cases of intoxication discharged from 0·2 per cent to 5·9 per cent of the defendants who appeared before them; five magistrates accounting for 14 per cent of the cases discharged from 8·9 per cent to 21·9 per cent of their cases; one judge discharged 34·9 per cent of his cases, and another, 78·9 per cent. The fact that out of the forty-one magistrates, thirty-nine whose case loads comprise 85 per cent of the cases of intoxication discharged from 0·2 per cent to 21·9 per cent of their respective cases indicates that the great majority of the magistrates do not differ unduly in their dispositions.

A more valid basis for the author's major conclusion is afforded by the data showing the percentages of the various kinds of penalties — suspended sentence, commitments to the workhouse or reformatory or city home, probation, good behaviour bond, and "others" — imposed for convictions of intoxication by each magistrate. Most of these dispositions are either suspensions, fines, or commitments to the workhouse. The major disparities are in the percentages of suspended sentences (7 to 83·2) and fines (6·6 to 61·4). It appears, too, that there is a pronounced negative association between the percentage of fines and the percentage of suspensions — the magistrates who impose a high percentage of fines accord relatively few suspensions. The range of variation in the percentages of commitments to the workhouse, 1·2 to 39·5, is not as great: thirty-three of the magistrates are within the range of 10·7 per cent to 39·5 per cent. An inspection of the data presented in graphic form suggests that if the suspensions and fines were

[1] *Ibid.*, p. 98.

combined, the differences among the judges in the proportions of sentences of imprisonment and non-imprisonment — taking into consideration individual differences in the cases — would not be excessively disparate.

Finally, the fact that intoxication is a very minor summary offence bearing a narrow range of legally permissible sanctions limits the usefulness of Everson's data in drawing inferences concerning disparities in sentencing criminal offenders.

Matthew F. McGuire and Alexander Holtzoff[1] cite examples of wide disparities among federal judges in sentencing liquor and narcotic cases. In liquor cases the average length of the prison sentences ranges between 40 days and 851 days; and in narcotic cases, between 31 days and 3,408 days. The variation in the proportions of the probations granted is likewise great. In one district during the fiscal year ending 30 June, 1939, 62·4 per cent of all convicted offenders were placed on probation while in another district only 4 per cent were thus penalized. The writers aver: "the conclusion seems inescapable that the differences are due primarily to diverse attitudes on the part of the individual judges toward various crimes and that the severity or lightness of the punishment depends in each instance very largely on the personality of the trial judge."[2] Although differences in attitudes among the individual judges unquestionably contribute to the differences in their sentences, the degree of their influence is problematic. The marked differences in sentences among the federal districts, each employing a number of judges, points with equal vigour to the alternative hypothesis that regional differences in attitudes toward certain crimes or in the availability or quality of probation facilities affects the sentencing practices of the judges.

Morris Ploscowe[3] quotes from the report of a New York Crime Commission which notes wide discrepancies in the sentences imposed upon offenders committed to the state penitentiary for the same offence. In cases of attempted burglary third degree the sentences range from 15 months to 5 years; in cases of burglary third degree, from 2 to 10 years; and in cases of robbery, from 7½ years to life. Data on variations in recidivism or on the circumstances surrounding the offence are not given.

[1] Matthew F. McGuire and Alexander Holtzoff, "The Problem of Sentencing in the Criminal Law," *Boston University Law Review*, CDXIII (1940), pp. 426–33.

[2] *Ibid.*, p. 428.

[3] Morris Ploscowe, "The Court and the Correctional System," *Contemporary Correction*, ed. Paul Tappan (New York: McGraw-Hill Book Co., Inc., 1951), p. 56.

Sam Bass Warner and Henry B. Cabot[1] present data on differences among eight district courts of Boston in the use of fines, probations, and jail sentences for all offences combined and for a few selected offences. The use of probation for all offences ranges from 11·1 per cent to 32·8 per cent and for larceny and breaking and entering, from 20 per cent to 46·5 per cent. Fines are assessed in the range of 19·4 per cent to 44·6 per cent for all cases; and from 7·3 per cent to 24·2 per cent for cases of larceny and breaking and entering. The range of the percentages of jail sentences for all cases is from 7·2 to 24·8; and for cases of larceny and breaking and entering, from 19·8 to 36·9.

The authors choose to attribute these variations to personality differences among the judges notwithstanding their awareness of the lack of experimental controls imposed upon their data. They state:

> Judges do not make the punishment fit the crime; neither do they make it fit the criminal, for as we have seen, in most cases they do not have sufficient information about him. It is possible, though we think not probable, that the variations have a rational basis. Different conditions in different parts of the city, different types of defendants, and different theories of sentencing among judges may be the explanation. On the other hand the variations may be due to personal idiosyncrasies of the judges.

Nevertheless, it is quite possible that differences in criminal behaviour patterns associated with differences in the populations of the various districts underlie the variations in the penalties. The failure to supply data on the distribution of offences or rates of recidivism according to the separate districts is a defect which precludes drawing any firm inferences concerning sentence variations.

Also, it is likely that the actual differences in sentences noted above are much less than the statistics indicate. Since these district courts are presumably inferior courts handling only minor offences, the length of the jail sentences is apt to be quite short.

The same authors also cite variations among Superior Court judges in the length of prison terms for armed robbery.[2] In the sixty-six cases studied there were thirty-one different terms ranging between 2½ to 3 years and 18 to 20 years. Information on the

[1] Sam Bass Warner and Henry B. Cabot, *Judges and Law Reform* (Cambridge: Harvard University Press, 1936), pp. 165-8.
[2] *Ibid.*, pp. 167-8.

number of judges involved and the distribution of sentences for each judge, as well as the circumstances of the crime and the recidivism of the offender is not noted. Such raw data provides limited warrant for generalization on the subject of disparities in sentences.

Harold E. Lane's study of variations in the sentences of penitentiary inmates[1] analyses the individual prison records of 1,661 criminals committed to the Massachusetts State Prison during a five-year period and arrives at the conclusion that at least 20 per cent received sentences which "... in the light of a careful social prognosis are indefensible".[2] A number of case studies are presented which, in Lane's opinion are heedlessly inconsistent with the requirements of justice: short sentences are often imposed upon professional habitual criminals and "relatively harmless, situational and occasional offenders" receive considerably longer sentences.

The premises which direct the organization and interpretation of the data are not those of jurisprudence but rather those of the positivist penology. Moreover, the case study documents were composed by correctional personnel whose interest in the offender is primarily rehabilitative; whereas the sentencing judge must balance a variety of objectives against one another. Hence information on the legal basis of the sentences is incomplete.

Lane summarizes two of the cases whose sentences strike him as being grossly inconsistent with the requirements of justice, one involving undue leniency and the other excessive severity. The first is the history of a man past sixty years of age who had spent 28 of the preceding 45 years in penal or correctional institutions. His prior criminal record discloses convictions for three burglaries, assault to rape, forgery, carnal abuse, and fourteen convictions of drunkenness. His present offence, for which he received a term of imprisonment of 2½ to 3 years, is the theft of women's dresses. The second case is that of a young offender who is reported as having a sickly childhood and only one prior conviction of a minor crime. He was sentenced to the state penitentiary for a term of 12 to 18 years for armed robbery and an additional term of 3 to 5 years for attempted armed robbery. His case study report states: "he appears to be a genuinely co-operative individual who speaks with

---

[1] Harold E. Lane, "Illogical Variations in Sentences of Felons Committed to Massachusetts State Prisons," *Journal of Criminal Law and Criminology*, XXXII (July–August 1941), pp. 171–90.

[2] *Ibid.*, p. 171.

regret of his offences and speaks frankly. He talks logically and with insight."[1] Although the young man has a less serious prior criminal record and makes a better impression on the case writer than the elderly social derelict, from a legal point of view there is an immense difference between the theft of dresses and robbery at gun point. Moreover, the impression of an offender which registers in the mind of a trial judge who hears the evidence concerning the criminal act and observes the offender during the trial may understandably differ from that received by a prison social worker.

In this study, again, the question of variation in community attitudes toward certain crimes and certain types of offenders is relevant inasmuch as the cases examined were sentenced in courts throughout the state.

The very few studies of variations in sentences among judges rotating in the same court provide a methodological advantage in that the influence of regional differences in attitudes toward various kinds of offences or offenders is presumably eliminated. The most widely cited and probably the most influential of all of the American studies of disparity in sentencing is Frederick J. Gaudet's analysis of individual differences in the sentencing practices of criminal court judges.[2] The data of this study consist of 7,442 cases of certain selected crimes tried within a ten-year period by six different judges serving in a county court of the state of New Jersey. The major conclusion of the study is that the criteria for sentencing are unevenly and capriciously applied; that the primary influence upon sentences is the personality of the judge — personality in the broad sense of social background, education, religion, experience on the bench, temperament, and social attitudes.

The primary basis for this induction is the finding that the judges differ radically among themselves in the application of four types of penalties: imprisonment, probation, fine, and suspended

---

[1] *Ibid.*, p. 182.

[2] Frederick J. Gaudet, "The Sentencing Behavior of the Judge," *Encyclopedia of Criminology*, eds. V. C. Branham and S. V. Kutash (New York: Philosophical Library, 1949), pp. 449–61; Frederick J. Gaudet, G. S. Harris and C. W. St. John, "Individual Differences in the Sentencing Tendencies of Judges," *Journal of Criminal Law and Criminology*, XXIII (January–February 1933), pp. 811–18; Frederick J. Gaudet, G. S. Harris and C. W. St. John, "Individual Differences in Penitentiary Sentences Given by Different Judges," *Journal of Applied Psychology*, VIII (October 1934), 675–80; Frederick J. Gaudet, "Individual Differences in the Sentencing Tendencies of Judges," *Archives of Psychology*, XXXII (1938); Frederick J. Gaudet, "The Differences Between Judges in the Granting of Sentences of Probation," *Temple Law Quarterly*, XIX (April 1946), pp. 471–84.

sentence. The range of variation among the judges in the percentage of each type of penalty imposed is as follows: imprisonment, 33·6 to 57·7; probations, 19·5 to 32·4; fines, 1·6 to 3·1; and suspensions, 15·7 to 33·8. When the variation in sentencing is examined within each of four offence categories, the disparities become even more pronounced.

The validity of the inference that the variations in sentencing are too great to be accounted for by differences in the gravity of the cases heard by the various judges hinges upon the assumption that since the cases were assigned to the judges by the district attorney's office on a rotational basis, by chance the case loads of the judges should be about the same with respect to the proportions of serious and minor crimes and the proportions of first offenders and recidivists. The method by which this assumption is verified, however, does not meet critical standards of experimental control.

The criterion by which Gaudet determines that the proportion of serious and minor crimes is the same for each judge is the proportionately equal distribution among the judges of each of four offence categories: sex crimes, property with violence, property, and violations of the state liquor laws. This criterion would be valid if, as Gaudet assumes, the four categories of offences, in the order named, represented a scale of gravity and the statutory penalties for the offences within each category were similar. This condition, however, is not adequately fulfilled. A check of the New Jersey statutes discloses that the ranges of the maximum sentences allowed for the crimes in three of the offence categories — sex, property with violence, and property — overlap one another to a marked degree.[1]

The category *property offences* comprising 82 per cent of the total cases spans as wide a range of variation in the maximum periods of imprisonment allowed by statute, 3 to 15 years, as does the entire classification of offences excluding the crime of rape for which the maximum penalty is 30 years. At the low end of the range is petit larceny, punishable by a maximum fine of $1,000 or a prison sentence of 3 years or both. At the high end is robbery, punishable by a maximum fine of $1,000 or a term of 15 years imprisonment or both. Sex crimes comprise only 9 per cent (692) of the cases. The statutory maxima of the prison sentences for these offences range from three years for adultery to thirty years for rape.

[1] Daniel T. O'Regan and Frank G. Schlosser, *The Criminal Laws of New Jersey*, Vol. 2 (New York: Baker, Voorhis and Co., Inc., 1942).

Accordingly, an unequal apportionment of the offences of various grades within either of these categories could contribute significantly to the sentencing variations noted. Since Gaudet does not provide information on the frequency of the individual crimes in each category or on their apportionment among the individual judges, we have no way of knowing in fact whether serious and minor crimes are equally distributed among the judges.

Even if it were established that the case loads of the individual judges contained equal proportions of offences of various statutory grades, we still could not assume that they are equivalent in the view of the court, for changes in the judicial evaluation of the seriousness of certain crimes may occur before or without benefit of legislation which recognizes changing attitudes toward certain crimes.[1] Thus crimes having about the same statutorily permissible penalty may elicit very different punitive reactions from the judges. A case in point is statutory rape, denoted "carnal abuse" in the New Jersey statutes. Although this offence carries a severe maximum penalty (15 years), it is commonly dealt with relatively leniently where the victim is of mature appearance and has been compliant. This tendency applies also to other sex crimes which though severely regarded in the statutes are leniently treated in the courts, particularly where the indiscretion involves the voluntary participation of two mature persons.

The assumption that there is no disproportion in the distribution of recidivists and non-recidivists among the case loads of the judges is based upon a study of a sample of 988 cases which yielded only 5·5 per cent recorded as having more than one prior offence. Gaudet does not state the source of the data on recidivism. Whether the information on prior convictions was entered into the records consulted as a matter of course or only incidentally is not clear. In either case, it appears that the information was unreliably reported. This is evidenced by an elaborating footnote stating that a considerable number of the defendants are probably repeaters ". . . but simply not recorded as such. Hence a study of these two classes of criminals (recidivists and non-recidivists) is hardly worth while on the basis of the data available".[2] The

---

[1] See Jerome Hall, *Theft, Law, and Society*, 2nd ed. (Indianapolis: the Bobbs-Merrill Co., 1952) which describes how cultural change moulding public opinion brought about the gradual mitigation of extremely harsh penalties for the crime of theft through judicial rather than legislative action.

[2] F. J. Gaudet, "Individual Differences in the Sentencing Tendencies of Judges," *op. cit.*, p. 11.

extremely low percentage of offenders with more than one prior offence casts further doubt on the validity of the data on recidivism. Another potential source of error is the classification of offenders according to whether they have two or more prior offences or less than two prior offences, for it is quite likely that judges distinguish much more finely among varying degrees of recidivism in sentencing. It is also possible that the nature of the prior offence(s) may affect the weight of the sentence.

In other less obvious ways, the bluntness of the controls imposed by Gaudet obscures certain subtle but important influences upon sentences. The sample of cases is biased in the direction of a disproportionate number of crimes of intermediate and high grades of seriousness because cases of ordinary misdemeanours such as assault and battery, gambling, bad checks, motor vehicle law violations, and the various crimes against the public, all tried in large numbers in courts at this level, are omitted from the study. With the exception of liquor law violations, accounting for only 3·5 per cent of the cases, petit larceny, a common offence, and adultery, infrequently a subject of criminal court action, the selected crimes of this analysis are high misdemeanours (felonies). It is precisely in the cases of more serious crimes for which the statutes provide relatively high maximum sentences that the greatest exercise of judicial discretion may occur in sentencing. Conversely, in sentencing cases of misdemeanours, discretion is considerably limited due to the relatively low ceiling on the penalties authorized by statute, and the disposition is apt to be more routine.

In short, Gaudet's analysis is insensitive to the scope and variability of the legal factors — the type of crime, the number of criminal acts charged, the circumstances of the crime, and the offender's past record — factors which may reasonably affect the judge's selection of a penalty.

A study of sentencing variations by Emil Frankel[1] published a few years after Gaudet's research and based upon criminal court data obtained in the same New Jersey county may be taken as a partial replication of Gaudet's investigation. Frankel compared the sentencing records of four judges comprising 4,029 cases. Although Frankel's data show some variation in the use of proba-

[1] Emil Frankel, "The offender and the Court: A Statistical Analysis of the Sentencing of Delinquents," *Journal of Criminal Law and Criminology*, XXXI (November–December 1940), pp. 448–56

tion — one of the judges gave considerably more sentences of probation than the others — there are no other marked differences. When the comparison between two of the judges who have enough cases for purposes of statistical analysis is controlled according to the type of crime and the number of charges against the offender, the resulting differences in sentences are negligible.[1]

Conclusions

The criticism of sentencing practices in the criminal courts shapes up into a two-pronged offensive: one line of attack thrusts at the system of criminal justice, and the other, at the allegedly erratic quality of justice dispensed by the system. The former is essentially a conflict of values engendered by opposing correctional philosophies; the latter involves primarily factual issues. The failure to separate these two quarrels — the failure to distinguish between justice in the law and justice before the law — has resulted in many unfounded assertions concerning the sentencing practices of judges. The crux of the error is that the criticism of sentencing practices is to a great extent deduced from objections to the system of criminal justice rather than induced from any sound factual basis.

This defect applies also to the formulation of research hypotheses, with the result that empirical studies of sentencing behaviour are segmental, betraying a lack of understanding of the juristic view of the criminal law as a normative science. Thus the complexity of the sentencing process, not to mention the process of human judgement, has been all but submerged in simplistic interpretations based upon fragmentary data. The neglect, in comparing the sentences of various groups of cases, to impose statistical controls appropriate to the subject of inquiry has resulted in a circularity of reasoning — the lack of proper and uniform criteria for sentencing is inferred from the disparities in sentences; and these in turn are attributed to the lack of adequate criteria.

[1] *Ibid.*, pp. 449–50.

II

METHODOLOGY

The Sample

The data of this study derive from the official court and police records of the city of Philadelphia, Pennsylvania. The research sample consists of the 1,437 convictions recorded in a volume of the docket of a non-jury prison court of the Philadelphia Court of Quarter Sessions. The cases were tried within a period of seventeen months during the years 1956–7.

The Quarter Sessions Courts are tribunals of county-wide criminal jurisdiction and are of two types: prison courts and bail courts. The fact that the defendants tried in prison court await trial under detention whereas those tried in bail court await trial at liberty under bond might imply that the former are of a generally lower socio-economic status than the latter and hence are at a disadvantage not only in raising bail bond but also in obtaining competent legal defence. However, a comparison of the cases of this study, all of which were tried in prison court, with a sample of 520 bail cases shows that the prison cases are charged with a higher proportion of serious offences for which bail bond is customarily high — 65 per cent of the prison cases but only 18·8 per cent of the bail cases involve convictions of felonies. This difference is reflected in the contrast between the two courts in the severity of the sentences imposed; only 15·1 per cent of the defendants convicted in bail court, compared to 78·4 per cent of those convicted in prison court receive prison sentences.

The prison cases are assigned to either a jury courtroom or a non-jury courtroom depending upon the plea at the arraignment. In the former, the defendants have pleaded not guilty at arraignment and have requested a jury trial; in the latter, the defendants have either pleaded guilty or have pleaded not guilty and have waived the right of trial by jury. The distinction is of little real consequence, however, since the great majority of defendants who are scheduled for jury trials at arraignment either change their pleas from not guilty to guilty or waive a jury trial after the trial commences. Out

21

of a sample of 94 cases tried in the jury room of the prison court, 89 of the defendants either changed their pleas to guilty or waived jury trial once the proceedings were under way. A reliable informant advised the writer that in many cases the change of plea or the waiver of a jury trial after the opening of the proceedings is due to the defence counsel's preference for the judge presiding in the jury room rather than the one in the non-jury room. By requesting a jury trial, the case can be brought before the favoured judge whereupon the plea can be changed to guilty or the right of a jury trial can be waived, the jury being excused for the remainder of the trial.

The Criteria for Sentencing

The information on each case given in the court docket comprises the date of the sentence, the date and serial number of the bills of indictment, the name of the judge, the name of the assistant district attorney prosecuting the case, the name of the defendant, the offence(s) charged in the indictment(s), the plea, the verdict, and the sentence. The heading of the police record file card contains the following information: name, age, sex, race, and address. On a form recently adopted, there are entries for the place of birth and citizenship status but this information is available only in a minority of cases. The body of the card gives the following information for each arrest: the date, the place, the offence charged, the date of trial, the level of the court disposing of the case — magistrate's court, municipal court, county court, federal court, or court martial — the presiding judge, and the disposition including the verdict and the sentence.

The above items are consolidated for purposes of this research into three sets of variables: legal factors, legally irrelevant factors, and factors in the criminal prosecution.

Legal factors include (*a*) the type of crime committed, (*b*) the number of bills of indictment on which the defendant is convicted, (*c*) the prior criminal record of the offender, and (*d*) the recommendations of auxiliary agencies of the court contained in reports of pre-sentence investigations and neuropsychiatric examinations.

Legally irrelevant factors consist of the biosocial traits of offenders that are recorded in police records. They include (*a*) sex, (*b*) age, (*c*) race, and (*d*) place of birth. Unfortunately, information on familial status or occupation is not provided.

Factors in the criminal prosecution include individual differences in the personnel participating in the trial — the judge and the assistant district attorney — and the type of plea entered by the defendant. The sources of the data do not report in all cases whether the defendant retained private counsel or was represented by the Voluntary Defender, a community agency providing free legal defence for those unable to pay. The available information indicates, however, that in the majority of cases counsel was furnished by the Voluntary Defender.

MEASURING THE SEVERITY OF SENTENCES

The relative severity of the different types of sentences is measured according to the degree of deprivation of civil freedom which they entail. Thus the various penalties in the order of their severity are: imprisonment, probation, fine, and suspended sentence. (No death penalties were imposed in any of the cases.)

Imprisonment

Pennsylvania law requires that prison sentences for crimes punishable by imprisonment "at labour by separate and solitary confinement" (imprisonment in a state penitentiary) be of indeterminate duration, the maximum of which shall be no more than the maximum penalty prescribed by statute[1] and the minimum, no more than one half of the maximum. The requirement of an indeterminate sentence does not apply to offenders convicted of crimes punishable by "simple imprisonment" (imprisonment in the county prison). Nevertheless, the sentences in such cases usually stipulate a minimum and a maximum term.

The measure of the severity of prison sentences adopted for purposes of this inquiry is the minimum term. This was decided in consultation with court officials who advised that it is a more realistic criterion than either the maximum or the median sentence, inasmuch as eligibility for parole commences with the expiration of the minimum term.

Prison sentences are herein classified according to whether the minimum term is 12 months or more, between 3 and 11½ months, or under 3 months. Most of the defendants who receive minima of 12 months or more are committed to the state penitentiary. These are guilty of crimes punishable by imprisonment at labour by

[1] 19 Purdon's Statutes 1057.

separate or solitary confinement. A small proportion of offenders convicted of such crimes are confined in the Philadelphia County Prison inasmuch as the Pennsylvania penal statutes authorize commitment to this correctional agency in lieu of the state penitentiary.[1] Offenders convicted of crimes punishable by simple imprisonment and sentenced to prison terms of 12 months or more also go to the county prison.

Included in the category of prison sentences with minima of 12 months or more are the pure indeterminate sentences to reformatories imposed upon a large proportion of male offenders under twenty-one years of age and nearly all of the females, since in import and duration this type of sentence equates with the penitentiary sentence. For the sake of brevity in reporting, sentences with minima of 12 months or more regardless of the place of commitment will be termed "penitentiary sentences".

Prison sentences having minimum terms between 3 and $11\frac{1}{2}$ months and less than 3 months are mostly commitments to the county prison, the remainder being confinements in the workhouse.

These three categories of prison sentences not only represent gradations in the severity of punishment but are related to differing procedures for releasing offenders on parole. Pennsylvania law provides that where a maximum term of imprisonment is 2 years or more, parole authority rests with the State Parole Board. Thus all offenders sentenced to a minimum term of at least 1 year must have a maximum term of at least 2 years, thereby bringing them under the authority of the State Parole Board. Where the maximum sentence is under 2 years — and in such cases the minimum must be less than 1 year[2] — parole power rests with the court in the form of a bench parole. In sentences having minima of less than 3 months, the minimum term is fixed at about the number of days spent in prison awaiting trial, and the maximum at no more than $23\frac{1}{2}$ months. The common procedure following the imposition of this type of sentence is the immediate or slightly delayed release of the offender on a parole issued from the bench. Although prison sentences in form, they are tantamount to sentences of probation in substance. The reasons given by the judges for imposing this

[1] 19 Purdon's Statutes 1021.

[2] Although the uppermost limit of the minimum in these cases could theoretically be just short of 1 year, custom fixes it at $11\frac{1}{2}$ months. There are no cases in the sample having minimum sentences between $11\frac{1}{2}$ and 12 months.

type of sentence rather than probation emphasize the sobering effect of a prison sentence upon the offender's attitude toward his misconduct.

Probation

Periods of probation range from 1 to 10 years. Probation is not punitive but rather treatment oriented. The judge's decision concerning the period of time to be spent on probation is presumably based upon an estimate of the offender's need for supervision rather than the gravity of the offence. Hence there is no breakdown of probation orders according to length.

Fines

Although the Pennsylvania Penal Code provides for the imposition of fines as an alternative sanction for most crimes and as a supplementary sanction for all crimes, sentences of fines alone at the Quarter Sessions Court level are generally imposed only for very minor offences such as liquor and lottery violations. The maximum amount of the fine prescribed by statute for each of the various crimes is relative to the degree of seriousness of the crime as measured by its maximum term of imprisonment.

Suspended sentence

Generally regarded as the mildest form of penalty, the suspended sentence may serve ends that do not betoken judicial leniency. In its mildest form, it serves as a judicial warning which establishes a criminal record for the offender. If he is again convicted, he risks the revocation of the suspension and the imposition of sentence. The judge may suspend sentence when an offender is wanted in another jurisdiction to face charges for a higher crime than the one of which he has been convicted. The suspended sentence may be employed in cases where a parolee who has been convicted of a crime is remanded to the penitentiary to serve out the unexpired portion of a previously imposed term of imprisonment. Instances of this type of disposition are tabulated in this study as penitentiary sentences rather than suspended sentences.

Since the proportion of cases disposed of by fines and suspended sentences is quite small, aggregating only 7·1 per cent of the total; and since there is virtually no difference between prison sentences with minima under 3 months and probation in the degree of restraint suffered by the convicted offender, these types of sentences will be combined in a number of instances into the category "non-imprisonment".

The fact that many of the cases are charged with more than one type of offence or penalized with more than one sentence poses problems in assigning cases to their proper categories. Consultation with court officials on the legal import of various combinations of charges and sentences resulted in the decision to adopt the following procedures.

(1) Where a case results in a conviction of more than one offence, the sentence is tabulated according to the highest crime.

(2) Where a case results in more than one type of sentence, such as imprisonment and fine or probation and fine, the tabulation is according to the more severe type of penalty.

(3) Where a case results in two or more prison sentences to run concurrently, the tabulation is according to the minimum of the longest sentence.

(4) Where a case results in two or more prison sentences to run consecutively, the tabulation is according to the sum of the minima.

THE STATISTICAL METHODS

The objective in the statistical analysis is to determine the degree to which the sentences differ according to variations in the criteria for sentencing. The nature of the data imposes certain limitations upon the type of statistical test which may be suitably applied. First, the various types of penalties are incommensurable in terms of some common unit of measurement. Although we can say that one type of penalty is more severe than another, it would be impossible to state objectively the length of a term of probation or the amount of a fine that would equate in punitive power, deterrent effect, or rehabilitative value with a given period of imprisonment. Even the terms of imprisonment are for a span of time rather than a fixed period. Secondly, the variables constituting the criteria for sentencing are all of a qualitative character.

It was decided, therefore, to employ statistical techniques whose models entail the least stringent requirements concerning the mathematical properties of the data to be analysed. With the exception of the analysis of sentencing variations among the judges, the chi-square (χ^2) test is used to test the hypothesis that two or more groups differ significantly with respect to the distribution of the penalties imposed.

Chi-square is a measure of the disparity between the frequencies which would occur in the various cells of a contingency table if there were complete independence between two variables (the theoretical frequencies) and the frequencies which do in fact occur (the observed frequencies). The theoretical frequency for each cell is obtained by multiplying the marginal totals of the row and the column and dividing the product by the total number of cases in the table.

The value of chi-square is obtained by dividing the square of the difference between the observed frequency and the theoretical frequency of each cell by the theoretical frequency and summing the results for all of the cells.[1] The greater the value of chi-square, the less the mathematical probability that the differences between the expected frequencies and the observed frequencies are due to chance, and the more significant the differences in penalties among the groups of cases compared.

The probabilities associated with varying values of chi-square for any number of "degrees of freedom", the number of cells in a table that are free to vary independently (calculated by multiplying the number of rows minus one by the number of columns minus one), are given in tabular form in any standard textbook on statistics. The rule is observed that in tables with more than one degree of freedom, fewer than 20 per cent of the cells may have an expected frequency of less than 5.

For testing the significance of the differences among the judges in sentences for cases of equivalent gravity, the Kruskal-Wallis one-way analysis of variance by ranks, or H-test,[2] is used. The chi-square test is not usually applicable to these experiments since the tables showing the distribution of the various types of sentences according to each judge contain more than 20 per cent of cells with theoretical frequencies of less than 5. It would have been possible, of course, to combine adjoining categories of sentences in order to increase the expected frequency in each cell, but this procedure might detract from the precision of the results.

In the H-test, the sentences of all of the cases are ranked ordinally in a single series. Then the ranks of the sentences of each judge are summed. The H-test enables us to determine the mathematical

---

[1] Chi-square $(\chi^2) = \Sigma \dfrac{(f_0 - f_t)^2}{f_t}$

[2] Sidney Siegel, *Non-parametric Statistics for the Behavioral Sciences* (New York: McGraw-Hill Book Co., Inc., 1956), pp. 184–93.

probability that the differences among the judges in the sums of their ranks could have occurred by chance. Where in the chi-square test the data are presented in the form of a contingency table involving as many sub-samples as there are types of penalties multiplied by the number of judges, in the H-test there are only as many sub-samples as there are judges.

The probabilities associated with various values of H are the same as for chi-square provided that there are more than five cases in each of the groups compared.

The criterion of statistical significance employed is the ·05 level of significance. In terms of our research objective, this signifies that if the differences in sentences between two or more categories of cases could have occurred by chance in no more than five times out of a hundred, we will infer that the differences in sentences are related to the antecedent variable according to which the cases are analysed.

III

LEGAL FACTORS IN SENTENCING

W<small>E</small> begin now the assessment of the relationship between each of the various criteria for sentencing and the severity of the sentences. This chapter will focus upon the effects of variables which are recognized by law as suitable measures of the gravity of a case: the nature of the offence, the extensiveness of the criminal activity charged, and the prior criminal record of the offender.

T<small>HE</small> C<small>RIME</small>

It was stated in Chapter I that the penal code supplies only a rough measure of the relative seriousness of different types of crimes; that the scale of offences implicit in the penal statutes is lacking in normative consistency, a number of trivial offences exceeding offences commonly regarded as grave threats to the public safety in the severity of the maximum penalty allowed by statute. It was also pointed out that the law grants the sentencing judge little guidance but much discretion to adjust the penalties in accordance with prevailing views of the relative seriousness of individual criminal acts.

Accordingly, in this phase of the inquiry questions are raised concerning the elements of criminal behaviour that evoke variation in the punitive reactions of the judges. What relative weights do the judges assign to the various interests protected by the criminal law? In property offences, is the worth of the stolen goods or the degree of premeditated calculation a factor? In crimes of violence, is the seriousness of the injury embodied in the criminal intent or actually inflicted a factor? Does the role of the victim in the criminal transaction bear any relationship to the severity of the sentences?

The pursuit of answers to these questions will take the form of an attempt to ferret out the scale of normative values underlying variation in the severity of the penalties imposed for different offences. Will this scale reflect the lack of normative consistency in the penal code; will it consist of a number of disconnected variables; or, will it exhibit a coherence in terms of some unifying value?

The procedure to be followed will consist, first, of locating the divergences between the rank order of the offences according to their statutory maximum penalties and their rank order according to the gravity of the sentences imposed, and then making explicit the differences in content between offences of adjoining rank order of gravity of punishment.

The classification of crimes

The 1,437 cases in the research sample involve convictions of 46 different offences. The classification of crimes employed for purposes of this inquiry complies with the requirement that each category be juridically authentic and include offences that are roughly equivalent with respect to the severity of the maximum penalty allowed by statute.

The broadest distinction in the gravity of crimes observed in the penal code of Pennsylvania is the classification of offences into the vaguely defined categories of felonies or misdemeanours.

> A felony is a heinous offence that is generally malum in se or an act that is bad in itself and against the laws of God, the nation, the state, or of nature. A felony is punishable by either death or imprisonment in the state penitentiary. *Commonwealth v. Strantz*, 137 Pa. Superior Ct. 448 (1939).
>
> All crimes less than felonies are misdemeanours. *Commonwealth ex. rel. Marsh v. Lindsey*, 130 Pa. Superior Ct. 448 (1938).[1]

The range of maximum prison terms allowed by statute for misdemeanours is from 1 month to 3 years; and for felonies from 5 years to life imprisonment or death.

Crimes of misdemeanour grade comprise about a third of the cases. They are assigned to three categories: crimes against the public, crimes against property, and crimes against the person. Offences against the public comprise a diversity of sub-categories: offences against public morals and decency, public peace, public justice, and public policy, economy and health.[2]

The felonies are assigned to six categories. The first is offences

---

[1] Theodore L. Reimel, *Pennsylvania Criminal Law Digest* (Philadelphia: George T. Bisel Co., 1944), p. v.

[2] A breakdown of each of these categories into its constituent offences appears in the Appendix, Table 1.

against personal property all of which involve the unlawful acquisition of property, or theft. It includes receiving stolen goods, larceny (subdivided in the analysis into larceny of auto and larceny of goods other than autos), burglary of a vehicle, fraud, and forgery. Each with the exception of forgery which allows a maximum sentence of 10 years' imprisonment provides for a maximum prison sentence of 5 years.

Burglary, a common law crime against the habitation for which the penal code permits a maximum term of 20 years, is the breaking or entering of real property with the intent to commit a felony. Since the felony usually intended and effected is theft, most indictments for burglary include additional counts for larceny and receiving stolen goods.

Robbery, embodying both the elements of a property crime and a crime against a person, is the unlawful taking of property by menace or force. There are two degrees of robbery in Pennsylvania. The graver offence punishable by a maximum term of 20 years' imprisonment includes one or a combination of the following elements: the use of an offensive weapon or instrument; complicity with the offender of one or more persons; and beating, striking, or ill using the victim. Robberies lacking these elements carry maximum penalties of 10 years' imprisonment. Since it can not always be determined from the docket entry which grade of robbery is charged, all cases of robbery are combined in one category.

Felonious crimes against the person are divided for purposes of analysis into two categories of gravity. The more serious category consists of offences bearing a maximum penalty of at least 10 years and includes first and second degree murder and voluntary manslaughter, rape, and assault with intent to rob. The lower category, consisting of crimes bearing maximum prison terms of 5 to 7 years' imprisonment, includes mayhem and assault with intent to kill, ravish, or maim.

Violation of the narcotic drug laws forbidding the illegal sale, use, or possession of narcotics is the only offence for which the legislature makes mandatory the imposition of a more severe penalty upon the averment of a prior conviction of a narcotics offence than for a first offence and for which a minimum term of imprisonment is specified by statute (2 years for a first offence). Therefore the maximum sentence of 5 years for a first offence tends to understate the legally defined gravity of narcotics violation relative to other offences.

Results

The statutory guide to the relative gravity of the various offences exerts a pronounced effect upon variations in sentences. Felony cases compared with misdemeanour cases receive proportionately three times as many penitentiary sentences (32·3 % : 10·3 %) but only half as many non-prison sentences (32·5 % : 61·9 %).[1]

There is also a high degree of correspondence between the order of categories of offences based upon the maximum sentence allowed by statute and the order based upon the severity of the sentences actually imposed.[2] The percentages of penitentiary sentences imposed for the various categories of offences listed in the order of their gravity according to statute are as follows:

Felonies

Crimes against the person	(10 years to life)	68·1%
Burglary	(20 years)	29·1%
Robbery	(10 to 20 years)	45·2%
Crimes against the person	(5 to 7 years)	61·3%
Narcotics violations	(5 years)	39·9%
Crimes against personal property	(5 years — except forgery: 10 years)	19·4%

Misdemeanours

Crimes against the person	(3 years)	14·9%
Property offences	(3 years)	15·7%
Offences against the public	(1 month to 3 years)	6·4%

The above figures show a number of inconsistencies between the rank order of the offences according to statute and their rank order according to the severity of the penalties imposed. Burglary according to statute rates higher than narcotics violations and felonious crimes against the person, except first and second degree murder, and equal to robbery; yet it ranks lower than any of the others in the severity of the penalties. The category felonious crimes against personal property has about equal statutory rank with narcotics violation and crimes of felonious assault but ranks much lower in the weight of the penalties imposed. Robbery, with a maximum statutory penalty of either 10 or 20 years is exceeded in the proportion of penitentiary sentences by the category crimes against the person with statutory maxima of only 5 to 7 years. We also find in a number of instances to be detailed in the ensuing

---

[1] Appendix, Table 2. [2] Appendix, Table 3.

analysis similar inconsistencies among different types of offences within the same category.

Turning to the task of determining what, if any, logic underlies these divergences, we find that the most salient factor determining the gradation of the offence categories according to the severity of the penalties is the degree of physical harm — potential or intended, threatened or actual — embodied in the offence. Ranking highest in the severity of the penalties imposed are the two categories of felonious crimes against the person. The statutory definitions of these offences assert the primacy of the intent to kill, maim, or otherwise physically injure the victim. The rank order of these offences according to the severity of the sentences follows generally their rank order based on the maximum statutory penalty.[1] All but one of the 25 cases of homicide (first and second degree murder and involuntary manslaughter) receive long terms in the penitentiary. Out of 34 cases of offences of felonious assault (assault to ravish or kill or rob and mayhem), 20, or 58·8 per cent, receive penitentiary sentences. The offence of rape, however, bearing a higher statutory maximum penalty (15 years) than any of the types of felonious assault or voluntary manslaughter, receives penitentiary sentences in only 38·5 per cent of cases. The reason, most likely, is that all of the rape cases are statutory rape involving sex relations voluntarily entered into by an underage "victim". Hence the elements of physical force or coercion and the intent to inflict injury are lacking.

Robbery, embodying the elements of a crime against both the person and property, ranks next after crimes against the person with 45·2 per cent of cases receiving penitentiary sentences. In this offence the threat or infliction of physical injury is secondary, or instrumental, to the unlawful acquisition of property. As has been stated, the records consulted do not consistently state the degree of robbery of which the defendant is convicted. However, in the instances where this information can be inferred, it appears that the higher degree of robbery which entails the use of a weapon or the complicity of two or more offenders, receives severer sentences.

The offences whose legal definitions lack the element of intent to commit bodily injury receive less severe penalties. The criteria by which the judges rank these offences are less apparent. Narcotics violations, usually the sale, use, or possession of drugs, rate next after robbery in the severity of sentences, 39·9 per cent of

[1] Appendix, Table 4.

c

cases resulting in commitments to the penitentiary. Although not denoted crimes against the person and not embodying any specific intent to inflict physical harm, by either the user upon himself or the vendor upon the vendee, they derive their enactment in large measure from the knowledge that drug addiction leads to harmful bodily effects and that the need for drugs or the influence of drugs is a precipitating factor in many crimes of violence.[1]

Burglary, defined as the breaking and entering of real property with intent to commit a felony, follows after narcotics violations with 29·1 per cent of cases committed to the penitentiary. Although the element of bodily injury or even face to face contact between the offender and his victim is not pertinent in the definition of burglary, it is, nevertheless, a crime which potentially involves personal contact between the offender and his victim, and accordingly, the possibility that the victim will suffer bodily harm at the hands of the offender.

The category offences against personal property ranks the lowest among the categories of felonious crimes in the percentage of penitentiary sentences imposed (19·4). The offences in this category involve neither bodily injury nor, except for fraud, personal contact between the offender and the victim. The penal code of Pennsylvania makes no provision for varying the maximum sentence of property offences according to the value of the stolen goods; it does not distinguish between petit larceny and grand larceny. Nor do the statutes grade these offences according to the method of theft. Except for forgery, punishable by a maximum sentence of 10 years' imprisonment, the maximum prison sentence for each of these crimes is 5 years.

Larceny of an auto, larceny, receiving stolen goods, and forgery are penalized quite uniformly, the percentages of penitentiary sentences meted out for these offences being 11·9, 16·9, 16·7, and 17·6, respectively, whereas the percentages of penitentiary sentences imposed for fraud and burglary of a vehicle are twice as great: 38·1 per cent and 32·4 per cent, respectively. Although the differences in sentences among all of these offences are not statistically significant[2] the cleavage between the first group of four offences and the second group of two offences in the percentages of penitentiary sentences imposed suggests questions concerning the

---

[1] Provisions of the Pennsylvania Penal Code relating to narcotics appear in Title 35 of Purdon's Statutes, annotated, *Health and Safety*.

[2] Appendix, Table 5.

nature of the standards by which the judges differentiate among offences in point of gravity. Does the greater severity in sentencing attendant upon convictions of fraud and burglary of a vehicle signify that the judges regard these offences as more reprehensible than the others; or is it a result of differences among these offences in factors extrinsic to the criminal act?

Considering first the latter question, it is possible of course that these sentence variations are due to differences among the offences in the criminal characteristics of the defendants who have committed them. The relatively mild penalties for larceny of an auto may be due to the fact that this offence is principally a crime of youth who are not as likely to have as lengthy prior criminal records as older offenders. Conversely, fraud which is penalized the heaviest of these crimes is more apt to be committed by older offenders who have undergone some degree of professionalization in crime and hence are more likely to have acquired more serious prior criminal records. Fraud is also apt to be a repetitive offence which raises the presumption that the sentences in cases of fraud are likely to be for convictions of several distinct violations charged in separate bills of indictment.

The data bearing on these suppositions are equivocal. The proportion of offenders having records of two or more prior convictions of felonies is the least in cases of auto theft; but receiving stolen goods, burglary of a vehicle, and fraud, each, contain a higher proportion of first felony offenders than auto theft.[1] Nor is the apparent leniency in sentencing extended to auto thieves likely to be due to their youthfulness *per se*; for, as will be demonstrated later, when differences in the rate of recidivism among offenders of different ages are controlled, the differences in sentences according to age are statistically non-significant.[2] We also find that forgery, receiving the second highest proportion of sentences of non-imprisonment, has the highest proportion of cases of recidivism; and fraud, presumably a professionalized crime, yields only to receiving stolen goods in the proportion of offenders with no prior felony convictions.[3]

Likewise, the data do not give credence to the supposition that the severity of the sentences meted out in fraud cases results from the relatively large number of violations of which defendants are convicted in a single court action.[4] Although fraud ranks next to

---

[1] Appendix, Table 6. [2] *Infra*, pp. 53–6.
[3] Appendix, Table 6. [4] Appendix, Table 7.

the highest in the percentage of cases charged in three or more bills of indictment (47·6), forgery which does not receive nearly as severe sentences, ranks the highest (58·9). Auto theft which involves convictions on more than one bill of indictment in proportionately more cases (84·7%) than any other personal property offence except forgery (88·2%) receives the lightest sentences.

Considering now the other alternative in interpreting the noticeably severe sentences for fraud and burglary of a vehicle — whether the judges view these offences as graver than the others — we have less in the way of objective evidence to guide us. One of the judges whose sentences contribute to the data of this analysis suggested that the degree of premeditation presumed to precede the criminal act is the explanation. True, the statutory definition of fraud implies an element of calculating deliberation not necessarily present in larceny which may be committed upon "sudden impulse". But this is no less true of forgery or receiving stolen goods each of which receives proportionately fewer than half as many penitentiary sentences as fraud.

To what, then, other than random variation, can we attribute these differences? The writer's guess with regard to burglary of a vehicle is that this crime may in the view of the judges partake of the qualities of burglary. Supporting this interpretation is the fact that there is close correspondence between the 309 cases of burglary and the 34 cases of burglary of a vehicle in the percentages of the various types of penalties imposed — penitentiary sentences, 29·1 : 32·4; prison sentences with minima between 3 and 11½ months, 39·5 : 35·2; and non-prison sentences, 31·4 : 35·2.

The interpretation we adduce to account for the notably heavier penalties for fraud is based upon a certain characteristic of this offence not shared by the other offences against personal property. Fraud is distinctive in that it involves the element of personal contact between the offender and the victim; the former engages the latter in a face to face relationship employing duplicity rather than stealth, as in other personal property crimes. This characteristic of fraud, the inter-personal contact between the offender and his victim, it is suggested, explains the higher position of this offence on the scale of penal sanctions than that held by burglary for which the law authorizes a much heavier maximum penalty.

There remains yet another question concerning the differences in penalties for property crimes. Despite the lack of statutory directions, do the judges vary their sentences for property crimes according to the value of the stolen goods? A comparison of the sentences for larceny of auto with those for larceny of other goods, assuming the generally higher value of autos, shows, contrary to expectation, little difference in the distribution of penalties.[1] Indeed, the auto thieves are committed to the penitentiary in only 11·9 per cent of cases compared with 16·9 per cent of the cases of thieves who steal less valuable goods. Likewise, a comparison of the sentences for burglary of a vehicle with those for larceny of auto points to the same answer. The former entails breaking into a motor car for the purpose of stealing articles; the latter entails stealing the vehicle including its contents. Yet as we have seen, convictions of burglary of a vehicle involve a much higher percentage of penitentiary sentences. It is possible, of course, though not likely, that the relative mildness of the sentences for auto theft compared to auto burglary is due to the comparatively high rate of recovery of stolen autos whereas other kinds of goods are more likely to have been converted. For this explanation to be plausible, the penalties for larceny (not of an auto) and receiving stolen goods should be about on a par with the penalties for burglary of a vehicle since these crimes are not likely to differ from burglary of a vehicle in the extent to which the stolen goods are either converted or recovered. Instead, they closely approximate the penalties for larceny of an auto.

Continuing the analysis, we find that the standards, discussed above, by which the judges gauge the relative seriousness of felonies are applied also to offences of misdemeanour grade.

The effect of the element of bodily injury is less apparent at the misdemeanour level. Even though cases of crimes against the person receive more than twice as great a percentage of prison sentences with minimum of 3 to 11½ months as cases of property crimes (45·9 : 19·1), the latter receives a slightly greater percentage of penitentiary sentences (15·7 : 14·9).[2] The court's estimate of the relative gravity of these two categories of offences is obscured by the fact that the property offences involve a much larger percentage of cases convicted of two or more separate violations (44·9 : 20·9); and a much greater percentage of recidivists (56·2 : 39·0). When these factors are held constant, the sentences for crimes against the person are clearly heavier than those for property crimes. In cases involving only one bill of indictment, 11·3 per cent of the cases of

[1] Appendix, Table 5.   [2] Appendix, Table 3.

crimes against the person and 7 per cent of the cases of property crimes receive penitentiary sentences; and in cases involving two bills of indictment, the percentages of penitentiary sentences are 26 and 18·8, respectively. In cases with no prior felony convictions, 14·6 per cent of the offenders convicted of crimes against the person compared to none of the offenders convicted of property crimes receive penitentiary sentences.

The sentences for offences against the public are on the whole much lighter than for the other categories of misdemeanours, only 6·4 per cent being prison sentences with minima of 12 months or more. An inspection of the differences in sentences among the offences constituting this category discloses a considerable range of variation in the proportion of penitentiary sentences imposed (0 % to 33 %). Interestingly, the penalties vary directly according to the extent to which the offence involves a specific victim. In crimes such as liquor and gambling violations, fornication, prostitution, etc., the victim is diffuse — "the public". Only 5 out of 156 (3·2 %) of these cases receive penitentiary sentences; 3 are chronic liquor law violators and one is a procurer with a string of prior convictions for the same offence. Carrying concealed weapons and driving intoxicated, offences which by their nature entail a potential physical threat to a possible victim, receive penitentiary sentences in 7·5 per cent of cases; and corrupting the morals of a minor, a crime which involves personal contact with a specific victim results in a higher proportion of penitentiary sentence (33 %) than any other misdemeanour except involuntary manslaughter.

The employment of the criteria applied to misdemeanours against the public is revealed in the sentences for the two felonious offences against the public, sodomy and solicitation to commit sodomy, the former punishable by a maximum prison sentence of 10 years and the latter, 5 years. Only 2 out of the 15 cases of these offences receive penitentiary sentences; and both of them entail convictions of the additional charge of currupting the morals of a minor. The criminal act in the remaining 13 cases involves mutuality between adults and hence no victim other than "the public".

Having disclosed the action of a number of factors in producing the differences in sentences among the various types of offences, we turn to the task of systematically drawing together the results of the analysis.

A revision of the preliminary classification of offences to constitute categories each containing offences that are closely similar with respect to statutory nature and the severity of penalties yields the following divisions arrayed in rank order of the percentage of penitentiary sentences imposed for each.

Felonies

Homicide	96·0
Felonious assault	58·5
Robbery	45·2
Narcotics violations	39·9
Statutory rape	38·4
Fraud	38·1
Burglary and burglary of a vehicle	29·4
Personal property (except fraud and burglary of a vehicle)	15·7

Misdemeanours

Offences against the person, including corrupting the morals of a minor	16·7
Property offences	15·7
Offences against the public	
Drunken driving, carrying concealed deadly weapons	7·5
Others	3·2

The above scale of offences suggests that the criteria by which the judges weigh the relative gravity of different forms of criminal behaviour consist of three interconnecting variables, each an aspect of the offender-victim relationship: the specificity of the victim, the degree of personal contact between the offender and the victim, and the degree of bodily injury involved in the criminal intent or in the criminal act. The first variable, the specificity of the victim, is continuous throughout the entire scale of offences. The second and third form separate scales for felonies and misdemeanours. The directness of the relationship between these variables, singly and jointly, and the severity of the sentences is depicted in Figure 1.

The specificity of the victim. The criterion of broadest scope is whether the victim of a crime is specific, such as an individual or a business, or diffuse, the "public". Where the victim is non-specific, as in crimes against the public, the penalties are least severe. However, certain crimes against the public which deviate from this criterion deviate also in the severity of the sentences. Carrying concealed deadly weapons and operating a motor vehicle intoxicated, offences which imply a potential specific victim, receive harsher sentences than other crimes in this category which rate as high a maximum penalty; and corrupting the morals of a minor, involving both a specific victim and personal contact between the offender and the victim, receives a much higher proportion of penitentiary sentences than any misdemeanour except involuntary manslaughter.

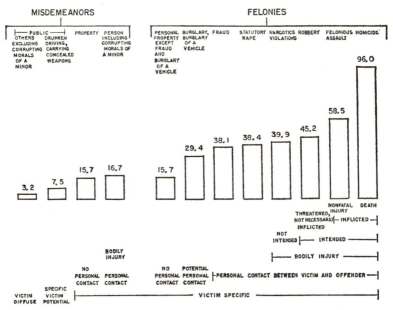

FIGURE I. OFFENCE CATEGORIES SCALED ACCORDING TO THE PERCENTAGE OF CASES RECEIVING PENITENTIARY SENTENCES AND THE DEGREE OF VIOLATION OF PERSONALITY.

The degree of personal contact between the offender and the victim. In cases where the victim is specific but the element of personal contact is not germane to the definition of the crime, as in offences against personal property except fraud, the penalties are heavier. Where direct contact with the victim is lacking but is a potentiality inherent in the nature of the offence, as in burglary, the sentences are more severe yet. Crimes incorporating the element of personal contact between the offender and his victim occupy a still higher position on the scale of gravity. Of these, fraud and statutory rape rank lowest and next to lowest, respectively. The former, as the denotation "statutory" implies, lacks the ingredient of coercion; the victim is a voluntary participant. In fraud, the perpetrator dupes the victim to achieve his end.

The degree of bodily injury. In offences containing the element of personal contact, the severity of the sentences varies directly with the extent to which the criminal intent or the criminal act embodies the element of bodily harm. The least heavily sentenced of offences involving physical injury is narcotics violations wherein bodily harm is presumed to be an inevitable by-product of the use of narcotics rather than a specific intent of the offender.[1] Robbery, ranking next higher, entails menace, coercion, or violence, but these elements are secondary to the intent to deprive the victim of his property. Where the essence of an offence is menace, coercion, or violence directed against the person of the victim, the penalties reach the highest point of severity.

The question now arises: Can the three criteria by which the judges measure the relative gravity of offences be assimilated to a variable of higher generality? In the writer's judgement, the moral value expressed by these criteria in the aggregate is the *inviolability of personality*. As Figure 1 shows, the offender-victim relationship in each type of offence receiving a higher percentage of penitentiary sentences than another, entails a greater degree of personalization along a gradient of the degree of bodily injury inflicted by the offender upon the victim. In essence, then, the standard underlying variation in the severity of the sentences imposed for diverse offences is the degree of *violation of personality*.

Thus it appears that the tendency toward increasing concern for the person and decreasing concern for property interests, initiated in nineteenth-century criminal legislation, is continuing but that legislation lags behind judicial administration in the expression of this tendency.

The Number of Bills of Indictment

The indictment is the legal document drawn up by the district attorney charging the defendant with the particular crime(s) of which he stands accused. The requirements of the Pennsylvania law for charging more than one criminal offence are, consistent with the right of the defendant, rather flexible. If two or more offences are part of the same criminal action they may be tried in

---

[1] Actually, the weight of the penalties for narcotics violations compared to statutory rape and fraud is much greater than the percentages of penitentiary sentences for these crimes would indicate. The average length of the penitentiary sentences for narcotics violations is considerably more than for either of the other offences.

separate counts of indictment. If the commission of a crime logically includes the commission of certain other crimes, they may be combined in one count of indictment. Rape, for example, may include assault with intent to ravish and assault and battery. The rationale for this procedure is that the evidence to be presented at the trial by the district attorney may indicate an acquittal of a higher charge but conviction of a lesser charge which may not be prosecuted without an indictment therefor. If, however, the accusation includes several separate unconnected offences, the practice of charging each in a separate bill of indictment is followed.

Thus the number of bills of indictment provides a measure of the extensiveness of the criminal activity with which an offender is charged. In cases involving convictions of two or more distinct separate offences, it is at the discretion of the judge to impose separate sentences for each to run concurrently or consecutively, or to impose one sentence for all of the convictions. In any case, the effect of this variable upon the severity of sentencing is quite pronounced. Defendants charged in one, two, three, and four or more bills of indictment, respectively, receive penitentiary sentences in the following percentages of cases: 15·2, 27·1, 40·4, and 57·8.[1] The strong relationship between the number of bills of indictments and the severity of the sentences occurs within each category of offences.

The Prior Criminal Record

The principle that a judge should consider an offender's prior criminal record in passing sentence is well established in the criminal law and broadly recognized in judicial custom. The penal code of Pennsylvania authorizes doubling the maximum penalty for certain crimes[2] upon the averment of a prior conviction of one of such crimes provided the latter offence is committed within 5 years of the former offence. Similarly, fourth offenders who have been convicted of such crimes may be sentenced to life imprisonment at the discretion of the judge upon a complaint filed by the district

---

[1] Appendix, Table 8.

[2] Treason, murder, voluntary manslaughter, sodomy, buggery, burglary, entering with intent to steal, robbery, arson, mayhem, kidnapping, sale of narcotics, perjury, abortion, pandering, incest, any offence employing a deadly weapon or explosive substance or corrosive fluid, or the attempt to commit any of the aforementioned crimes (18 Purdon's Statutes 5108).

attorney followed by a hearing to determine that the accused is the person named in the prior convictions averred and an examination of the offender's life history. These statutory provisions are invoked rarely in the Pennsylvania courts and in none of the cases of this study. Nevertheless, the data forcefully demonstrate that up to the limits of the maximum sentences allowed by statute for the various offences, the judges differentiate according to the quantity and enormity of the offender's past convictions.

The variables by which we shall investigate the effect of the prior criminal record upon variation in the severity of sentences are as follows: (1) the number of convictions which includes (a) the number of convictions of felonies and (b) the number of convictions of misdemeanours; (2) the severity of the sentences for prior convictions; (3) the number of arrests; (4) the recency of the last prior conviction.

Results

Prior convictions

There is a marked relationship between this factor and variation in the severity of the sentences, the percentage of penitentiary sentences ranging from 12·6 for cases with no prior convictions to 34·7 for cases with 4 or more prior convictions, and the percentage of non-prison sentences (probation, suspensions, fines, and bench paroles) ranging from 65·9 for cases with no prior convictions to 12·3 for cases with 4 or more prior convictions.

In order to determine if the judges vary their sentences according to the grade of the prior offence, we hold constant the number of prior felony convictions while investigating the relationship between the number of prior convictions of misdemeanours and the severity of the sentence. The results indicate that only in cases involving no prior felony convictions does variation in the number of prior misdemeanour convictions significantly affect the sentencing of the court ($P < 0.001$).[1] Within the categories of cases containing 1, 2, 3, and 4 or more prior convictions of felonies there is no tendency whatever for increases in the number of prior convictions of misdemeanours to produce heavier penalties. The number of prior convictions of felonies, however, exerts a strikingly significant effect upon variation in the severity of the sentences ($P < 0.001$); the percentage of penitentiary sentences in each of

[1] Appendix, Table 9.

the categories of this variable is as follows: none, 14·4; one, 27; two, 35·5; three, 31·5; and four or more, 50·7.[1]

The above findings do not indicate whether the judges take as their principal measure of the gravity of the prior offence the grade of the crime involved or the severity of its sentence inasmuch as both of these factors are closely related. In order to determine if the gravity of the penalties received for prior convictions exerts an independent effect upon the severity of the sentences, the number of prior convictions of felonies is held constant while investigating the relationship between the number of prior convictions resulting in penitentiary sentences and the weight of the penalties. Except, again, within the category "no prior convictions of felonies", the association between the two variables is not statistically significant.[2]

The results in cases having no prior convictions of felonies which show that the severity of the sentences varies with both the number of misdemeanour convictions resulting in penitentiary sentences and the number of convictions of misdemeanours regardless of their sentences raise the question: Do prior misdemeanours disposed of by mild penalties exert as much effect upon sentence variations as misdemeanours disposed of by heavy penalties? Holding constant the number of prior misdemeanour convictions resulting in penitentiary sentences, we find that only in cases having no prior convictions resulting in penitentiary sentences does the mere number of prior convictions of misdemeanours exert a significant effect upon variations in the gravity of the sentences.[3]

Prior arrests not resulting in conviction

Does the mere bulk of the defendant's prior record influence the weight of the sentences? Many convicted offenders have prior records listing dozens of arrests, very often for petty charges which have eventuated in diverse numbers of convictions. Arrests not resulting in conviction are not technically a part of the prior criminal record but a careless perusal of the file cards by the judges could result in unduly harsh sentences for the offender with many arrests even though few resulted in conviction. It is also possible that the judges might take the attitude "where there's smoke, there's fire" and sentence accordingly.

An analysis of the relationship between the number of prior arrests not resulting in conviction and the severity of the sentences,

[1] Appendix, Table 10.   [2] Appendix, Table 11.   [3] Appendix, Table 12.

holding constant the number of prior convictions, yields an extremely high probability that the two variables are independent of one another.[1] Indeed, the various categories of the number of prior arrests are practically identical with respect to the proportional distribution of the different types of sentences.

The recency of the last prior conviction

The time interval between the present conviction and the preceding conviction may provide a rough measure of a recidivist's attempt to work out a law-abiding adjustment after an earlier clash with the law.[2] Presumably those who have been lately convicted have not yet "learned a lesson". Of course, it is perhaps just as likely that those who have not been convicted for a relatively long period have either managed to elude capture or if arrested, were not convicted.

The hypothesis that judges vary the severity of their sentences according to the recency of the last prior conviction is tested by comparing the sentences of three groups of recidivists whose last prior felony convictions occurred at different time intervals prior to the present conviction: 0 to 2 years ago, 3 to 4 years ago, and 5 or more years ago. Since the defendants in each successive group have a somewhat lower percentage of cases with more than one prior felony conviction (62·6 : 55·8 : 49·3), separate comparisons are made within different categories of recidivism: cases with one, two, three, and four or more prior felony convictions. Although the results of these statistical experiments taken singly do not affirm the hypothesis, none of them yielding differences that are statistically significant,[3] there is an increasing tendency as the number of prior felony convictions increases for judges to impose more severe sentences on those most recently convicted. In cases with one prior felony conviction, offenders convicted within 0 to 2 years following a previous felony conviction, compared with offenders whose last prior conviction occurred 3 to 4 years ago or 5 or more years ago, receive about the same percentage of penitentiary sentences (26·5 : 31·9 : 25) but somewhat fewer sentences of non-imprisonment (30·4% : 34·8% : 42·1%). However, in cases involving four or more prior felony convictions, the most recently convicted defendants receive a considerably larger percentage of penitentiary

[1] Appendix, Table 13.
[2] National Probation and Parole Association, *op. cit.*, p. 41.
[3] Appendix, Table 14.

sentences (60·8 : 42·1 : 47·3), and a much smaller percentage of sentences of non-imprisonment (9·8 : 26·3 : 30·9).

It is questionable, however, that this sentencing tendency reflects ire or impatience with offenders who have failed to reform — although the judges may indeed experience this reaction. The data as a whole point more directly to the interpretation that the offender with a long prior record who has suffered a previous conviction within 2 years prior to the present conviction is more apt to be a parole violator than one whose last prior conviction dates back 3 or more years; and in cases involving a parole violation, the judge usually incorporates into the sentence an additional penalty representing the unexpired portion of a previously imposed penitentiary sentence.

To summarize, the various measures of recidivism which are available to the judge do not contribute equally to the weight of the sentences. The degree of influence of each is relative to its importance in the law. The number of prior convictions of felonies takes precedence as a determinant of the severity of the sentences. In cases with at least one prior felony conviction, neither the number of prior misdemeanour convictions nor the severity of the sentences for prior misdemeanour convictions produces any appreciable variation in sentences. In cases with no prior felony convictions, the number of prior misdemeanour convictions resulting in penitentiary sentences is invoked as a criterion for sentencing; and in cases lacking prior convictions of either felonies or misdemeanours disposed of by penitentiary sentences, the number of prior convictions of misdemeanours disposed of by milder penalties (non-prison sentences and prison sentences with minima between 3 and 11½ months), becomes a significant factor. The recency of the last prior felony conviction is a factor of little significance and the number of arrests not resulting in conviction is a factor of no significance whatever. In short, the judges tend to employ the highest criterion which is applicable to a case ignoring those which are lesser or irrelevant.

Analysis of the Criteria of the Length of Penitentiary Sentences

For the sake of brevity, the term penitentiary sentence has been employed to refer to prison sentences with minima of 12 months or more, whether commitments to the state penitentiary or the county prison, and pure indeterminate sentences. The great breadth of the range of these sentences, a few of which are as high as life imprisonment, points up the desirability of a separate analysis for this group of cases. The categories of length into which the penitentiary sentences are divided are as follows: 12 to 23 months, 24 to 35 months, 36 to 59 months, and 60 or more months. The pure indeterminate sentences are included in the category 12 to 23 months.

RESULTS

The rank order of the gravity of the offences with respect to the length of the penitentiary sentence imposed is almost identical to the rank order based upon the type of penalty imposed.[1] The percentage of the penitentiary sentences in each offence category with minimum terms of no less than 3 years is as follows:

Felonies
Person (maximum sentence 10 years to life)	56·3%
Robbery	44·3%
Narcotics	32·4%
Burglary	25·6%
Person (maximum sentence 5 to 7 years)	10·5%
Personal property	10·0%

Misdemeanours
Person	10·0%
Property	0·0%
Public	0·0%

The only shift in rank is the drop in the position of offences against the person, maximum penalty 5 to 7 years, from next to the most severely sanctioned category to next to the least — a change which is due primarily to the rather low statutory maxima allowed for these offences.

The prior criminal record and the number of bills of indictment do not exert the same effect upon variation in the length of the penitentiary sentences as upon variation in the type of sentences. The influence of variation in the degree of recidivism is slight and far from statistically significant ($P > 0·30$).[2] Defendants with less than 2, 2 to 3, and 4 or more prior felony convictions receive penitentiary sentences with minimum terms of three years or more in

---

[1] Appendix, Table 15.   [1] Appendix, Table 16.

24 per cent, 23·6 per cent and 31·5 per cent of cases, respectively. This might imply that as the case becomes more serious the prior criminal record of the offender is of less concern to the sentencing judge. But that is not precisely the explanation, for the judge may have already considered the prior record in deciding to impose a penitentiary sentence. Where there are aggravating circumstances in the commission of an offence, the judges tend to sentence close to or right up to the hilt of the maximum penalty allowed by statute, leaving themselves little latitude to adjust the penalty according to the gravity of the prior criminal record.

The number of bills of indictment on which the offender is convicted manifests a significant effect upon the length of penitentiary sentences.[1] Defendants charged in 1 to 2, 3 to 4, and 5 or more bills, respectively, receive sentences with minima of 5 years or more in the following percentages of cases: 10·3, 14·6, and 26·7. This relationship holds within each offence category except felonious crimes against the person and misdemeanours. Here, again, is evidence that as the offence becomes more serious, the judges tend to press to the maximum penalty, thus limiting the possible effect of other factors which may be considered in mitigation or aggravation of the penalty.

SUMMARY AND CONCLUSIONS

In summary the results of this investigation contradict the widely held notion that there are no standards, or at best vague ones, by which criminal court judges sentence convicted defendants. Not only do the legal criteria for sentencing impose definite restraints upon the judge but in their reciprocal action reveal the operation of orderly processes which flow reasonably from the penal philosophy implicit in the criminal law.

The rank order of the various offence categories according to the severity of the sentence imposed corresponds closely but not entirely to their rank order based upon the statutory maximum penalties. The deviations of the former from the latter do not appear to be without logic. They involve offences whose statutory penalties are unrealistic in the light of present day normative standards — petty crimes punishable by as severe penalties as very serious crimes or crimes which in the passage of time have acquired new meanings, not as yet incorporated into legislation, which define

[1] Appendix, Table 17.

them as greater or lesser threats to the public safety than formerly. The sentencing of the court reflects an impatience with the inherent conservatism of the formal law and a striving to redefine the gravity of certain crimes in accord with the spirit of the time through judicial administration. The paramount value, it appears, around which the reorganization of penal values is taking place is the *inviolability of personality*. There is a direct relationship between the severity of the sentences and the extent to which the victim is specific, there is interpersonal contact between the offender and the victim, and bodily injury is intended or inflicted by the offender.

The number of separate unconnected offences of which the defendant is convicted, measured by the number of bills of indictment in the accusation, exerts a powerful influence upon variation in the severity of the sentences.

The relative influence of each of the variables constituting the prior criminal record corrresponds to its legally recognized importance. The most influential element is the number of prior convictions of felonies. In cases with one or more prior felony convictions, past convictions of misdemeanours have no significant effect upon variations in sentences. In cases with no prior felony conviction, the number of prior convictions resulting in penitentiary sentences becomes a significant factor. In cases involving no prior felony convictions and no prior misdemeanour convictions resulting in penitentiary sentences, the severity of the sentences varies significantly according to the number of misdemeanours disposed of by lesser penalties. The recency of the last prior felony conviction has a slight though not significant effect upon sentencing and the number of arrests not resulting in conviction has no effect whatever.

The analysis of variation in the length of the penitentiary sentences indicates that as the cases mount in gravity, the offence becomes increasingly the paramount criterion for sentencing and the effect of the prior record declines to a point of negligibility. Variation in the number of bills of indictment exerts a significant but decreasing effect as the offence approaches maximum seriousness.

All in all, the findings reveal a keen sensitivity on the part of the court to differences in the legal make-up of the cases. The cumulative effect of the offence, the number of bills of indictment, and the prior record upon the distribution of the various types of penalties is depicted in Figure 2 on the following page.

D

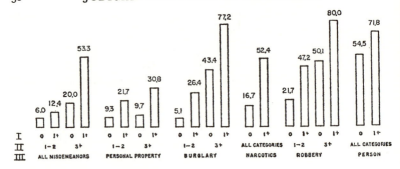

KEY: I   NUMBER OF PRIOR FELONY CONVICTIONS.
     II   NUMBER OF BILLS OF INDICTMENT.
     III   OFFENCE.

FIGURE 2.   PERCENTAGE OF CASES RECEIVING PENITENTIARY SENTENCES IN EACH OFFENCE CATEGORY STRATIFIED ACCORDING TO THE NUMBER OF BILLS OF INDICTMENT AND THE NUMBER OF PRIOR FELONY CONVICTIONS.

IV

NON-LEGAL FACTORS IN SENTENCING

THE preceding chapter has demonstrated the highly restrictive effect of legal criteria upon the sentences meted out to criminal offenders. The results, however, do not eliminate the possibility that biases incompatible with the goals of justice affect the deliberations of the sentencing judge. Indeed, the presumption prevails in the literature of criminology and jurisprudence that these at least as much as legal criteria determine the sentence a judge imposes.[1] This chapter will focus upon the question: Within the limitations imposed by the legal criteria, to what degree, if any, is variability in sentencing determined by legally irrelevant criteria?

The information given on all cases in the official records limits the exploration of the effects of non-legal factors to sex, race, and age. A form adopted in 1956 for the recording of police records includes an entry for place of birth and citizenship but information on these items is available in only a portion of the cases. In the instances where citizenship is stated, nearly all of the defendants are United States citizens. The addresses of the defendants indicate that the vast majority of them reside in poorer class neighbourhoods. Consequently an analysis of differences in sentences according to residence and citizenship is not worthwhile.

SEX

Do protective attitudes toward women affect the severity of the penalties meted out to female defendants? Studies of the criminality of women have revealed sexual differences in patterns of criminal behaviour accompanied by differences in rates of arrest and prosecution, the females receiving generally more leniency at the hands of the law.[2] The fact that females constitute only 91 or 6·3 per cent of the cases may reflect that there is a favourable bias toward

---

[1] *Supra*, pp. 6–7.

[2] Otto Pollak, *The Criminality of Women* (Philadelphia: The University of Pennsylvania Press, 1949).

women that results in proportionately fewer female cases eventually going to trial; or it may indicate that for cultural and biological reasons women are not as criminally inclined as men.

A comparison of the penalties imposed upon male and female defendants would seem to support the view that chivalric attitudes, or at least a tendency to react more in the spirit of rehabilitation rather than punitively toward women, enter into the administration of criminal justice.[1] The women receive a much larger proportion of pure indeterminate sentences than the men (14·1 % : 1·5 %) but a much smaller percentage of penitentiary sentences with minimum and maximum limits (6·5 : 23·4). These differences do not, however, betoken an attitude of greater leniency toward women since there is no statutory provision for the pure indeterminate sentence for men over 21 years of age.[2] Although there are differences in release procedures between the pure indeterminate sentence and the penitentiary sentence, the former entails at least the equivalent minimum term of the latter. When the two categories are combined the proportions amount to 24·9 per cent for men and 20·6 per cent for women. The men receive a much larger percentage of prison sentences with minima between 3 and 11½ months (33·3 : 21·7) and a much smaller percentage of sentences of non-imprisonment (41·8 : 57·7). The difference in the percentage of probations is quite marked: 23·9 for women and 13·9 for men.

Vitiating the force of these findings is the fact that the male and female cases differ significantly in rates of recidivism and in the distribution of the various types of offences.[3] Felonies account for 63·7 per cent of the male offences compared with 54·4 per cent of the female offences. At the felony level, a slightly higher percentage of females is convicted of crimes against the person (8·7 : 5·6) and a slightly smaller percentage is convicted of robbery (7·6 : 9·5). About the same percentage of females as males is convicted of personal property crimes (19·6 : 21·6). Proportionately three times as many females are convicted of narcotics violation (15·2 % : 5·9 %), but only one-seventh as many females are convicted of burglary (3·3 % : 22·8 %). At the misdemeanour level, the female cases involve a much higher proportion of the pettiest offences

---

[1] Appendix, Table 18.

[2] Since 1952, offenders convicted of certain sex crimes may be sentenced to an indeterminate sentence of one day to life imprisonment (19 Purdon's Statutes 1166). This provision of the penal code was not applied to any of the cases of this study.

[3] Appendix, Table 19.

such as prostitution and liquor violations, crimes for which the maximum penalties are the lightest.

The recidivism of the females is only about half of that of the males: 25·3 per cent of the females compared with 53·7 per cent of the males have one or more prior convictions of felonies.

A comparison of the two sexes in cases with no prior convictions of a felony with the grade of the offence controlled yields results[1] affirming the equality of the sexes before the criminal law. In felony cases the males and the females receive practically the same percentages of penitentiary sentences (20·1 : 20·7), prison sentences with minima of 3 to 11½ months (31·7 : 27·6), and non-prison sentences (48·2 : 51·7). In misdemeanour cases the women fare slightly though not significantly better than the men receiving smaller percentages of penitentiary sentences (5·3 : 7) and prison sentences with minima of 3 to 11½ months (15·8 : 23·3) and a larger percentage of non-prison sentences (78·9 : 69·7).

AGE

It is commonly believed that youthful offenders receive greater leniency in court than older offenders because they arouse paternal sentiments within the judge. The reverse is equally plausible, however, on the basis that judges are likely to have more sympathy with the older defendants. What are the facts?

The age-groups according to which the effect of age is analysed — under 21, 21 to 29, and 30 or over — are empirically derived, preliminary investigation having shown that the boundaries of these age brackets mark the points at which significant changes in the severity of the sentences occur. The lower limit of the under 21 group is 18 years of age with the exception of one case of a 16-year-old charged with murder. A further breakdown of the 30 and over age-group is needless, since the differences in penalties between offenders age 30 to 39 and those age 40 and over is negligible (P> 0·80).

A comparison of the three age-groups shows that the defendants under 21 receive noticeably lighter penalties than either of the older groups.[2] Each successively older group receives a slightly higher percentage of penitentiary sentences than the one preceding it (22·9 : 24·4 : 25·5). With reference to prison sentences with minima between 3 and 11½ months, the 21 to 29 group receives the

---

[1] Appendix, Table 20.   [2] Appendix, Table 21.

highest percentage (36·8) followed by the over 29 group (30·4) which in turn exceeds the under 21 group (26·3). The percentage of non-prison sentences received in each of the age-groups going from the youngest to the oldest is as follows: 50·8, 38·8, and 44·1.

These figures, however, are misleading in their implications; for there are marked differences among the three age-groups in the variables which constitute the legal criteria for sentencing. As one might expect, there is a close relationship between age and recidivism.[1] Only 11·7 per cent of the defendants under 21 have more than one prior felony conviction compared with 25·7 per cent of those 21 to 29 and 29 per cent of those over 29.

We note also that there are highly significant differences among the three age-groups in the distribution of the types of offences. The cases of the youngest group contain a somewhat larger percentage of felonies than those of either the 21 to 29 group or the over 29 group (74·1 : 69·3 : 57·1).[2] The differences in the percentage of felonious crimes against the person, proceeding from the youngest to the oldest group, are slight (5·8 : 3·8 : 8·1), but the percentages of robberies differ markedly, the lower the age, the greater the percentage of robberies (19 : 11·3 : 4). The data in cases of robbery suggest that the robbery techniques of the offenders under 21 tend more toward "strong arm" methods or "purse-snatchings", whereas those age 21 to 29 are more prone to rob at gunpoint. Offenders in both the under 21 and 21 to 29 group commit more burglaries than those over 29 (22·9% : 25% : 17·7%). Narcotics violations are relatively few in the youngest group and highest in the middle group (2% : 8·6% : 5·9%). The percentage of crimes against personal property is about the same in each successively older age-bracket (24·4% : 21% : 21·4%).

An additional factor intervening between age and the severity of the penalties is variation in the number of bills of indictment in the accusation — the younger the offender, the greater the probability that he will be convicted of two or more separate offences. This is particularly true with respect to crimes requiring strength and agility, such as burglary and robbery. In cases of burglary with no prior felony conviction, 75 per cent of the offenders under 21 are convicted on two or more bills of indictment compared with 43·5 per cent of those age 21 to 29, and 30 per cent of those over 29 years of age. In cases of robbery with no prior felony conviction, 80·8 per cent of the defendants under 21 compared with 68·8 per

---

[1] Appendix, Table 22.　　　　[2] Appendix, Table 23.

cent of those 21 or over are convicted on two or more bills of indictment.

Having noted the differences in the patterns of criminal behaviour among the three age-groups, we are now in a position to assess more accurately the affect of age upon the severity of sentencing.

A comparison of the penalties received by the three age-groups in 120 burglary cases with no prior felony conviction yields differences that are not statistically significant (P> 0·20).[1] In contrast, however, to the results obtained in the comparison involving all of the cases, there is a pronounced decline in the percentage of penitentiary sentences with increasing age — from 17·8 to 11·3 to 6·7. Also the oldest group receives a higher percentage of non-prison sentences (66·6) than either the youngest (57·2) or the intermediate group (54·8). When we recall that there is a sharply decreasing proportion of cases with two or more bills of indictment in each successively older age-group, these differences in sentences are about what we should expect them to be on the assumption that there is no age bias in sentencing. The likelihood of this assumption is put to a more stringent test by introducing the additional control of *number of bills of indictment*. A comparison of the sentences of the offenders under 30 years of age with those of the offenders age 30 or over in cases involving one bill of indictment shows that only 1 out of the 42 cases in the younger group and 2 out of the 29 cases in the older group receive penitentiary sentences — a difference which is too slight to indicate a trend.

A similar analysis of the cases of robbery with no prior felony convictions comparing the sentences of offenders under 21 with those 21 and over also yields differences in sentences that are statistically non-significant (P> 0·20).[2] The younger group receives a slightly higher percentage of penitentiary sentences than the older group (34·6 : 31·3), a noticeably smaller percentage of prison sentences with minima between 3 and 11½ months (26·7 : 45·8), and a higher percentage of sentences of non-imprisonment (38·7 : 22·9). In at least partial explanation of these differences are the facts, already noted, that a greater proportion of the younger robbers are charged generally with more separate offences than the older offenders but tend to commit the less serious variety of robbery. Also, a greater proportion of the under 21 group have no prior convictions of misdemeanours (65·4 % : 50·0 %).

[1] Appendix, Table 24.   [2] Appendix, Table 25.

In another analysis involving 52 cases of aggravated assault and battery with no prior felony conviction we compare the 29 cases of defendants under 30 with the 23 cases of defendants 30 or over. The results indicate a very high probability that the differences in sentences are not significant $(P > 0.70)$.[1] Here, the younger offenders receive a somewhat smaller percentage of penitentiary sentences ($13.8 : 21.8$), about the same percentage of sentences with minima of 3 to $11\frac{1}{2}$ months ($41.4 : 39.1$), and a slightly higher percentage of sentences of non-imprisonment ($44.8 : 39.1$).

To sum up, the findings demonstrate that *age differences in patterns of criminal behaviour* rather than age *per se* produces the variations in sentences among different age-groups.

RACE

The ratio of Negro defendants to white defendants in the research sample is 3.3 to 1, the two groups numbering $1,092$ and 333, respectively. Twelve cases including 9 classified as Puerto Rican, 1 as Chinese, and 2 without information on race are omitted from the analysis.

A comparison of the penalties imposed upon the two separate racial groups would seem to indicate that the white defendants are favoured with somewhat milder penalties than the Negro defendants.[2] The whites receive a slightly higher percentage of penitentiary sentences ($26.1 : 24.3$) but a somewhat lower percentage of prison sentences with minima between 3 and $11\frac{1}{2}$ months ($27.9 : 33.9$). Both races receive identical percentages of prison sentences with minima of less than three months (21.3). A major difference is in the allocation of probations, whites receiving this disposition in nearly twice the percentage of cases as Negroes ($20.1 : 12.8$). The whites yield to the Negroes in the percentage of fines ($1.5 : 4.9$) and are about equal to the Negroes in the percentage of suspended sentences ($3.1 : 2.8$).

Although the statistical probability of differences as great as these occurring by chance is less than one out of a hundred, the actual difference in the severity of the penalties is moderate. If we sum for each race the percentages of the types of non-prison sentences, the resulting totals are virtually equal: 39 for whites and 42.9 for Negroes. Again, comparing the two races — this time

---

[1] Appendix, Table 26.   [2] Appendix, Table 27.

combining the sentences of non-imprisonment — we find that the differences in sentences are not great enough (P > ·10) to meet the criterion of statistical significance.

If we could assume that the white and Negro cases are equivalent with respect to the distribution of offences and the rate of recidivism, this phase of the analysis might terminate here. The data, however, reveal that the two races differ markedly with respect to patterns of criminal behaviour and the development of criminal careers in relation to age. First we note that the white defendants, on the average, are younger than the Negro defendants. The percentages of white and Negro defendants in each age-bracket are as follows: under 21, 20·2 and 12·6; 21 to 29, 40·5 and 45·1; over 29, 39·3 and 42·3.[1] These age differences imply not only differences between the races in rates of recidivism but also differences in the distribution of the various offence categories. Indeed in the under 21 age-bracket there is a pronounced difference between the races in the proportions of the various types of crimes — a difference which tends to diminish as the offenders of both races mount in age.[2] In the youngest age-group, the Negroes compared with the whites are charged, proportionately, with more than two and a half times as many robberies (24·1 % : 8·9 %), more than twice as many felonious crimes against the person (7·3 % : 3 %), but only half as many burglaries (16·1 % : 35·8 %). In both the intermediate and highest age-groups, the two races draw more closely together with respect to the percentage distribution of crimes; the major difference in the former is in the much larger proportion of Negroes who are convicted of narcotics violations (10·2 % : 2·2 %). The offences most highly associated with race differences are liquor and gambling violations — 96 per cent of these offences are committed by the Negroes, 77·7 per cent by Negroes in the over 29 age-group.

Going from the youngest to the eldest age-category, certain parallel tendencies occur in both racial groups — the proportions of felonious crimes against the person and the proportions of misdemeanours increase and the proportions of burglaries decrease. Oddly the percentage of theft is higher for Negroes than for whites in the under 21 age-bracket (26·2 : 20·9) but lower in the 21 to 29 (19·3 : 27·4) and 30 and over (19·1 : 30·2) age-brackets.

Having determined the major differences between the white and Negro cases with respect to the variables constituting the legal

[1] Appendix, Table 28.   [2] Appendix, Table 29.

criteria for sentencing, we proceed now to test the hypothesis that the court practises racial discrimination.

Considering first race differences in sentences for burglary, we find that the whites receive generally milder penalties than the Negroes. Although the former receive a slightly higher percentage of penitentiary sentences (31·1 : 28·6), they receive, proportionately, fewer prison sentences with minima between 3 and 11½ months (31·1 : 42·9) and more non-prison sentences (37·8 : 28·6).

It will be recalled that in the under 21 age-bracket a much larger percentage of whites than Negroes are convicted of burglary (35·8 : 16·1).[1] From the same data we can readily calculate that 27·2 per cent of the white burglars are under 21 years of age, as against only 10 per cent of the Negro burglars. Hence the latter are likely to have a higher rate of recidivism. A comparison of white and Negro defendants in cases of burglary with no prior felony convictions indicates very slight differences in the distribution of sentences (P > 0·80).[2] The percentages of whites and Negroes receiving each type of penalty are as follows: penitentiary sentences, 10·8 and 13·3; prison sentences with minima between 3 and 11½ months, 29·7 and 30·1; prison sentences with minima of less than 3 months, 27 and 32·5; probations, 32·5 and 24·1. When the last two categories of penalties are combined as "non-imprisonment", the differences in sentences between the two races become even slighter.

In burglary cases with one or more prior felony convictions, race differences in sentences are non-significant but to a lesser degree (P > 0·10).[3] The white defendants receive a higher percentage of penitentiary sentences (45·3 : 38·1), a much lower percentage of prison sentences with minima between 3 and 11½ months (32·1 : 50·1), and twice the percentage of non-prison sentences (22·6 : 11·1). In view, however, of the less rigorous control for recidivism imposed in this comparison than in the preceding one, the actual differences are likely to be much less than indicated.

The results of similar analyses in cases of robbery with 0 to 1 prior felony convictions (P > 0·50),[4] theft with 0 to 1 prior felony convictions (P > 0·30),[5] and theft with 2 or more prior felony convictions (P > 0·10),[6] and misdemeanours exclusive of liquor and

---

[1] Appendix, Table 29.   [2] Appendix, Table 30.
[3] Appendix, Table 30.   [4] Appendix, Table 31.
[5] Appendix, Table 32.   [6] Appendix, Table 32.

gambling violations (P> 0·20)[1] show no evidences of racial discrimination in sentencing.

A control of race differences in the proportions of cases charged in various numbers of bills of indictment reduces the difference between the races in the severity of the penalties even more. In cases of theft and burglary combined with no prior felony conviction charged in 1 to 2 bills of indictment, the percentages of white and Negro cases in each category of penalties are almost equal: penitentiary sentences, 8·2 and 7; prison sentences with minima of 3 and 11½ months, 28·6 and 31·5; non-imprisonment, 63·2 and 61·5.

Although the foregoing analyses yield no statistically significant difference between whites and Negroes in the severity of the penalties, certain differences linked with race repeatedly occur in the distribution of sentences. The whites generally receive a larger proportion of penitentiary sentences, a smaller proportion of sentences with minima between 3 and 11½ months and a greater portion of probations.

Does the higher percentage of penitentiary sentences imposed upon the white defendants reflect the judicial attitude that white citizens should be held to a more rigid standard of responsible conduct? Does the higher percentage of probations granted to the white offenders reflect a belief on the part of the courts that a greater emphasis should be placed on reformation with respect to them than to Negro delinquents?

The answer to each of these questions is no. The most likely explanation of the difference in the percentage of penitentiary sentences is the fact that white defendants are convicted on more than one bill of indictment to a much greater extent than the Negroes (55·2 % : 34·9 %).

Figures on probation alone do not provide an accurate index to the judge's willingness to seek rehabilitative goals in sentencing. The number of prison sentences with minima under 3 months must also be considered. This disposition, it has been explained, is in effect the same as probation inasmuch as the defendant is released on a bench parole following the imposition of the sentence and the supervision of the defendant is administered by the probation department of the court. In the more rigorously controlled comparisons of the races — those involving no prior felony convictions or crimes with low maximum penalties — whites and

[1] Appendix, Table 33.

Negroes differ very little in the combined percentages of probations and sentences with minimum under 3 months. For burglary, whites receive these penalties in 59·5 per cent of cases, and Negroes, in 56·6 per cent of cases; for misdemeanours, the percentages are 50 for whites and 50·8 for Negroes; and for offences against personal property, the percentages are 58·6 and 54, respectively.

The question may persist in the mind of the reader: Granted that there is no practical difference in penal effect between a prison sentence followed immediately by parole and probation, why do whites get more probations than Negroes?

The answer lies in certain differences between the white and Negro cases — differences in their legal make-up which are relevant to the conditions for probation.

The original grant of discretion to the court to impose sentences of probation was given by the Act of 1909 (10 May, P.L. 495) which states:[1]

> Whenever any person shall be convicted in any court of this Commonwealth of any crime, except murder, administering poison, kidnapping, incest, sodomy, rape, assault with intent to rape, arson or burglary of a dwelling-house, and it does not appear to the said court that the defendant has ever been in prison for crime, either in this State or elsewhere, and where the said court believes that the character of the defendant and the circumstances of the case such that he or she is not likely again to engage in an offensive course of conduct, and that the public good does not demand or require that the defendant should suffer the penalty imposed by law, the said court shall have the power to suspend the imposing of sentence and place the defendant on probation.

Later legislation[2] broadened the power of the judge to grant probation by eliminating the restrictions on the type of crime and prior imprisonment; otherwise, the wording is almost identical to the Law of 1909 quoted above. Where the original law provided some specific criteria for determining that the public welfare would not suffer by failure to punish the offender, the present law permits the judge almost complete freedom in making the determination. Nevertheless, it appears that most of the cases accorded probation comply with the standards set forth in the earlier law. The characteristics of the 209 cases granted probation are as follows: 151 (72·2%) are cases having no prior felony convictions;

[1] 19 Purdon's Statutes 1081.   [2] The Act of 1941 (6 August, P.L. 861).

170 (81·3%) involve minor offences: misdemeanours, felonious crimes against personal property, and burglary; and 126 (62·9%) are offenders in these three crime categories who have no prior felony convictions. Clearly, then, the customary criteria for probation, in the absence of specific statutory directives, are that the offence be minor and that the offender's past record does not indicate a criminal pattern.

The data indicate that the white defendants to a much greater extent than the Negro defendants meet these standards for probation. A much larger percentage of whites than Negroes is in the under 21 age-group (20·2 : 12·6). This age category although comprising only 14·3 per cent of the cases receives 24·4 per cent of the probations.[1] Within this age-group, the Negroes commit comparatively many more crimes involving bodily harm or the threat of bodily harm than the whites — crimes against the person and robbery combined account for 31·4 per cent of the Negro cases compared with 11·9 per cent of the white cases. In the 21 to 29 and over 29 age-groups, as well, the Negroes exceed the whites in the percentage of offences for which probation is seldom granted.

Therefore, in order to put the issue of racial discrimination in the granting of probations to a valid test, the comparison of the sentences of white and Negro defendants is limited to cases of minor seriousness — misdemeanours and felonious crimes against personal property committed by first offenders. The results are statistically non-significant (P > 0·20).[2] The difference in the proportions of probations is practically nil, the whites receiving this disposition in 27·9 per cent of cases and the Negroes, in 30·3 per cent of cases. The differences with respect to the other types of penalties, however, indicate a trend toward greater leniency for the Negro defendants[3] who receive a much smaller percentage of penitentiary sentences (3·6 : 11·9) and a much larger percentage of non-prison sentences (79·4 : 67·4). This difference should not be interpreted to mean that in cases of minor crimes, the judges are more clement with Negro offenders; rather it reflects that the Negro cases of misdemeanours involve a much higher proportion of the pettiest offences, liquor and gambling violations, than the white cases.

Finally, we consider the effect of racial differences upon the length of penitentiary sentences. The results of the analysis show that it is negligible (P > 0·50),[4] the white defendants receiving

[1] Appendix, Table 21.   [2] Appendix, Table 34.
[3] Appendix, Table 34.   [4] Appendix, Table 35.

proportionately slightly fewer sentences with minima of 5 years or more (11·8% : 15·3%) but slightly more sentences with minima of 3 to 5 years (14·1 : 10·1). The difference in the percentages of sentences with minima of 2 to 3 years imposed upon whites and Negroes is virtually nil (16·5 : 17·9) as is the difference in sentences with minima of 1 to 2 years (57·6 : 56·7).[1]

PLACE OF BIRTH

Do the judges in sentencing favour defendants native to the locality of the court over those who are migrants? Do they consciously or unconsciously inject a social class bias into their sentencing?

The data do not provide the necessary information to make a direct test of the latter question but an indirect probe is possible. On the assumption that Northern-born Negroes are generally more assimilated to the norms of middle-class white society, presumably the judges' cultural orientation, than Southern-born Negroes, we should expect the judges to favour the former in their sentencing. Or, on the assumption that judges are more tolerant of the miscreancy of Southern-born Negroes because they haven't yet learned to adjust to the ways of urban industrial society, we should expect them to be more lenient with this group. The data bear out neither assumption. Information on the place of birth is available in 303 of the Negro cases. A comparison of the sentences of the Northern-born Negroes, the vast majority of them native to Philadelphia, with those of Negroes born in segregationist states does not turn up any appreciable differences between the two groups (P> 0·50).[2]

It is interesting to note that the percentages of the various types of sentences received by the Northern-born Negroes are almost precisely intermediate in magnitude to those received by the whites and Southern-born Negroes.[3] This suggests that the Northern-born Negro defendants are in process of assimilation to the criminal behaviour patterns of the local whites.

---

[1] These findings contradict a major conclusion of Lemert and Rosberg's study cited earlier — that "race prejudice is a more significantly operating variable when the groups concerned are definitely stereotyped as criminal". Lemert and Rosberg, *op. cit.*, p. 19.

[2] Appendix, Table 36.

[3] Appendix, Table 37.

Summary

The preliminary investigation of differences in sentences according to sex, age, and race indicates that females are favoured as compared with males, younger offenders as compared with older offenders, and whites as compared with Negroes. Intensive analysis reveals, however, that these variations in the gravity of the penalties are due to differences in criminal behaviour patterns associated with these biosocial variables, not to hidden prejudice. The female defendants commit fewer serious crimes and have a lower rate of recidivism than the male defendants. Increasing age is accompanied by a rise in recidivism but a decline in the proportion of convictions of the more serious types of crimes. White and Negro defendants differ considerably in age-cycles in criminal behaviour patterns. Youthful Negro defendants commit a much higher proportion of crimes of violence than youthful white defendants. As the two racial groups increase in age, their patterns of criminal behaviour tend to become more similar.

When the effect of these variant patterns of criminal behaviour is controlled by comparing different categories of defendants in cases that are similar with respect to the offence and the prior criminal record, the differences in the severity of the sentences become negligible.

The hypothesis that the judges discriminate between Northern-born Negroes and Southern-born Negroes in sentencing fails to stand. The proportions of the various penalties received by the Northern-born Negroes are intermediate in magnitude to those received by the whites and the Southern-born Negroes. This, coupled with the finding which shows that Negro patterns of criminality tend to approximate white patterns of criminality as offenders in the two groups increase in age, is interpreted to mean that the Negro offenders are in process of assimilation to white patterns of criminality.

If differences in penalties according to the variables sex, age, race, and place of birth are an indication of judicial prejudice, the conclusion is inescapable that the judges of the court in which these cases were tried are free of any such bias in their sentencing.

V

THE PREDICTION OF SENTENCES

THE high degree of relationship between the severity of the sentences and each of the legal criteria for sentencing — the gravity of the offence, the number of separate criminal transactions, and the number of prior felony convictions — prompts the idea of utilizing these factors in the construction of an index that would measure the relative gravity of the various cases and have actuarial validity in predicting the sentences that judges will impose. Also by rendering all of the cases commensurable, such an index would facilitate an investigation of the degree of consistency among the judges in sentencing cases of equivalent gravity.

The first step in the construction of a prediction table — the establishment of those factors which have the greatest association with variations in the type of penalties — has already been taken. Since it is essential that the predictive factors utilized be independent of one another in their effects upon variations in the sentences, before proceeding we must ascertain if the interrelationships among them are statistically significant. We find that variation in the number of bills of indictment is independent of variation in the number of prior felony convictions $(P > 0.50)$[1] but that each of these factors varies significantly with differences in the offence categories. The percentage of cases involving three or more bills of indictment is as low as 3·7 in misdemeanours against the person and as high as 39·3 in robbery.[2] Ranking the highest in the percentage of cases involving two or more prior felony convictions is narcotics violations (48·3) followed by burglary (36·9) and theft (35·9), with misdemeanours against the public ranking the lowest (17·9).[3]

The failure to control the effect of the interaction between the type of crime and each of the other criteria in developing an index would tend to exaggerate the weight assigned to those offences which are more repetitive or more commonly committed by recidivists. Conversely it would tend to minimize the weight as-

[1] Appendix, Table 38.   [2] Appendix, Table 39.   [3] Appendix, Table 40.

signed to those crimes committed in smaller proportion by recidivists or charged generally in fewer bills of indictment.

These distortive effects are precluded by determining separately for each offence category the weight to be assigned to the various sub-categories of the number of bills of indictment and the number of prior felony convictions.

The next step is the weighting of the various sub-categories of the predictive factors relative to the differences among them in the severity of the sentences. The numerical value of the weight assigned to each sub-category is based upon the following procedure. Values of 30, 20, and 10, respectively, are accorded to penitentiary sentences, prison sentences with minima between 3 and $11\frac{1}{2}$ months, and to sentences of nonimprisonment. Then the mean of the values of the sentences in each category of the predictive variables is determined to the nearest whole number. The score of a case is the sum of the two appropriate means — one for the sub-category of the number of bills of indictment and the other for the sub-category of the number of prior felony convictions in the particular offence category into which the case falls. The method is illustrated below in cases of burglary with one bill of indictment and no prior felony conviction.

	1 Indictment			0 Prior felony conviction		
	No. of Cases (1)	Value (2)	(1) . (2)	No. of Cases (1)	Value (2)	(1) . (2)
Prison: 12 months and up ..	27	30	810	15	30	450
Prison: 3–11½ months ..	60	20	1,200	36	20	720
Non-imprisonment	61	10	610	70	10	700
Total	148		2,620	121		1,870

Wtd. Mean = 17·7(18)   Wtd. Mean = 15·4(15)
Score for cases of burglary with 1 bill of indictment and no prior felony conviction = 33(18 + 15).

The possible range of the scores is from 20 to 60 although none of the cases quite achieves these extremes; the actual range of the scores is from 23 to 58. The proportions of penitentiary sentences for the various values of the index ranges from 3·4 per cent in the 297 cases scoring under 30 to 90·6 per cent in the 53 cases scoring over 49.[1] The two major points of inflection in the distribution of

[1] Appendix, Table 41.

E

the sentences occur at about equal intervals on the continuum of scores, yielding three score categories: 23 to 35, 36 to 44, and 45 to 58 comprising 697, 537, and 203 cases, respectively. The percentages of the various types of penalties in each of the three categories are as follows:

	45–58	36–44	23–35
Penitentiary: 12 months and up	69·5	30·3	7·2
Prison: 3–11½ months	19·7	45·3	26·5
Non-imprisonment	10·8	24·4	66·3
Total	100·0	100·0	100·0

The above figures show that defendants with scores of 23 to 35 have only seven chances out of a hundred of receiving a penitentiary sentence and a better than even chance (sixty-six chances out of a hundred) of not serving a prison sentence. Defendants with scores of 45 to 58, on the other hand, suffer the risk of receiving penitentiary sentences in seventy chances out of a hundred and have only eleven chances out of a hundred of receiving less than a prison sentence.

Although a statistical table for the prediction of the severity of sentences may have little practical value, except perhaps to criminals who wish to anticipate the consequences of a possible conviction, it possesses the scientific value of enabling one to perceive in concise form the determining effect of the legal criteria upon the severity of the sentences. Also by demonstrating the strong capacity of the index to discriminate among the cases according to the gravity of their sentences,[1] it prepares the way for the task of the next chapter — the investigation of differences among the judges in sentencing cases of equivalent gravity.

[1] C (coefficient of contingency) = 0·503; P < 0·001. (See Appendix, Table 42.) The upper limit of C in a 3 × 3 table is 0·816.

VI

FACTORS IN THE CRIMINAL PROSECUTION

THUS far the investigation has focused upon the offence and its perpetrator. In this chapter, variations in penalties will be analysed according to differences in the court personnel — the judge, the prosecutor — and the type of plea: guilty or not guilty.

DIFFERENCES AMONG THE JUDGES IN THE SEVERITY OF SENTENCES

The data of other studies of the sentencing process is harnessed to the proposition that the personality and social background of the individual judge determine his sentencing tendencies. The present study, *per contra*, puts forward the hypothesis that certain elements of the professional role of the judge — norms rooted in law, judicial precedent, and the mores — have a restraining effect upon individual differences in penal philosophy, social background, or idiosyncrasies which affect the judges' attitudes toward various classes of offenders; particularly where the judges preside in the same court, hold membership in the same local bar, and, presumably, have practised law in the same locality prior to ascending to the bench. Therefore we should expect the judges to agree as well as differ in sentencing cases of equal gravity. The ensuing analysis will attempt to uncover the degree of consistency among the judges in sentencing and the circumstances under which it varies.

Since the precise point at which consistency shades off into inconsistency is apt to be a debatable question fraught with semantic difficulties, the criterion of consistency must be arbitrary. Accordingly, the determination of the degree of consistency in sentencing cases of equivalent gravity will be based upon the following procedures. First, the sentences are ranked with respect to severity. Then, applying the Kruskal-Wallis one way analysis of variance,[1] we test the hypothesis that there is no significant

[1] Sidney Siegel, *op. cit.*, pp. 184–93.

difference among the average ranks of the various judges. If the probability that differences as great as those observed would occur by chance is no more than five out of a hundred times ($P \leqslant 0\cdot05$), we shall conclude that there is undue disparity in sentencing.

The cases of the research sample are distributed in various proportions among 21 judges; 16 are members of the Philadelphia Court of Common Pleas and 5 are visiting judges from courts of equal jurisdictional rank in nearby counties.

Considering first all of the cases, we find that the variation among the judges in the percentage of each type of penalty is quite great.[1] Judge "D" imposes only one penitentiary sentence in 26 cases ($3\cdot8\%$); at the other extreme, Judge "R" imposes penitentiary sentences in 10 out of 19 cases ($52\cdot6\%$). This discrepancy does not appear so flagrant, however, upon noting that "D", the lenient judge, has proportionately only one-third as many cases in the high score category (45 to 58) as Judge "R" ($7\cdot7\% : 21\cdot1\%$).

A comparison of the judges within each of the score categories yields differences in sentences that are great enough to meet the criterion of inconsistency. The degree of the disparity, however, is not uniform among the three categories of cases; it is most pronounced in cases at an intermediate level of gravity and tapers off in cases at either a high or low level of gravity.

In the 23 to 35 score category, the judges divide into two groups.[2] The larger group consists of 12 judges who impose non-prison sentences in from 60 per cent to $82\cdot4$ per cent of their respective case loads. The six judges in the other group tend to be more stringent, imposing such sentences in from $29\cdot7$ per cent to 50 per cent of their cases. The statistical probability that differences in sentences as great as those observed in the first group would occur by chance is more than thirty out of a hundred times, and in the smaller group, more than twenty out of a hundred times. Thus within each group the differences are not great enough to warrant the inference of inconsistency in sentencing.

In the cases scoring 36 to 44, the judges divide into three groups.[3] Three judges impose penitentiary sentences in from 0 per cent to $11\cdot8$ per cent of cases; 8 judges, from $18\cdot4$ per cent to $34\cdot2$ per cent of cases; and 6 judges from 38 per cent to $57\cdot1$ per cent of cases. One judge, "R", actually a composite of four of the visiting judges, metes out penitentiary sentences in 80 per cent of his cases. Since the cases tried by "R" number only five, they are included with

---

[1] Appendix, Table 43.   [2] Appendix, Table 44.   [3] Appendix, Table 45.

the third group. Within each of these groups, the differences in sentences are not statistically significant (P> 0·30; P> 0·70; P> 0·10).

In the cases scoring 45 to 58, the major division occurs between the 14 judges each of whom imposes penitentiary sentences in more than half of his cases and the 4 judges who assess such penalties in less than half of their respective cases.[1] In neither group are the differences in sentences among the judges statistically significant (P> 50; P> 30).

The question arises: Do the judges tend to retain approximately the relative rank order of severity in cases of different levels of gravity? In general, yes.[2] Seven of the judges rank within the same third, upper or middle or lower, within each of the score categories; and another 7 rank in the same third in two out of the three score categories.

To summarize, there appears to be less inconsistency among the judges in the types of penalties imposed for the most serious and the least serious cases. In cases of minor gravity, the sentences of 6 of the judges are so rigorous as to be out of line with the sentences of the other 12. In the most serious cases, 4 of the judges tend to be much more lenient than the others. The greatest disparity in sentencing occurs in the cases of intermediate gravity. Here, the differences in sentencing are so great that the judges can be assimilated to no fewer than three groups — numbering 3, 8, and 7 — within which there are no significant differences in sentences.

Thus we conclude that when cases are patently either mild or grave, the standards for sentencing are clearly structured and generally shared by the judges. As the cases move from the extreme of gravity or mildness toward intermediacy, judicial standards tend to become less stable and sentencing increasingly reflects the individuality of the judge.

DIFFERENCES AMONG THE JUDGES IN THE LENGTH OF PENITENTIARY SENTENCES

A common complaint has it that disparities in the length of penitentiary sentences imposed upon convicted felons contribute to prison riots, disturbances, and other morale problems affecting the administration of penal institutions. Since the major premise of this judgement derives from the rebellious inmate's explanation of his intractability, and since he is unlikely to possess either suffi-

---

[1] Appendix, Table 46.   [2] W(coefficient of concordance) = 0·59.

cient information or the emotional detachment to make a valid estimate of the severity of his sentence relative to that of other inmates whose crimes and past records are on a par with his own, the substance of the complaint is problematic.

In this stage of the inquiry we shall test the hypothesis that judges rotating in the same court are unduly disparate in the length of the penitentiary sentences they award.

The development of an index by which to measure the seriousness of the cases disposed of by penitentiary sentences entails essentially the same rationale as that involved in the index based upon variations in the types of penalties. They differ, however, in the predictive variables utilized. Earlier it was shown that there is no association between the length of the minimum penitentiary sentence and the number of prior felony convictions; that the significant criteria are the offence and the number of bills of indictment. The latter, however, has no effect upon the length of penitentiary sentences in felonious crimes against the person and in misdemeanours. Accordingly, except for the cases within these two offence categories, the scores are based upon the distribution of the sentences in each offence category stratified according to the categories of the number of bills of indictment. The scores for misdemeanours and felonious crimes against the person are calculated without reference to the number of bills of indictment.

The sentences are assigned values of 10, 20, 30 or 40 depending upon whether their minima are 12 to 23 months, 24 to 35 months, 36 to 59 months, or over 59 months. The procedure for scoring each case is the same as illustrated in the preceding chapter for scoring cases according to the gravity of the types of penalties.[1]

The scores obtained by this method range from 10 to 35. The percentage distribution of the different terms of imprisonment according to the magnitude of the score is given in condensed form as follows:

	24–35	17–23	10–16
5 or more years	46·0	14·0	3·0
2–5 years ..	28·6	43·0	18·2
1–2 years ..	25·4	43·0	78·8
Total ..	100·0	100·0	100·0

The above figures attest to the high degree of discriminative power of the index $(P < 0.001; C = 0.47)$.[2]

[1] *Supra*, p. 65.   [2] Appendix, Table 47.

The degree of consistency among the judges in the length of the penitentiary sentences imposed is investigated within two score categories, 10 to 22 and 23 to 35, the former consisting of 240 cases and the latter, of 114 cases. The results show a surprising degree of uniformity in sentencing. The differences in the cases of lesser gravity are not statistically significant $(P>0.10)$,[1] none of the judges inflicting sentences with minima between 12 and 23 months in fewer than 50 per cent of cases. In the cases of greater seriousness, the differences are barely significant $(0.02<P<0.05)$, the percentage of sentences with minima between 12 and 23 months imposed by each judge with the exception of Judge "I" ranging from 22.2 per cent to 57.1 per cent. "I" is clearly harsher than the others; out of his 8 cases in this score category, 5 were sentenced to serve minimum terms of 5 years or more and 3 were given minima of 36–59 months. On eliminating his case load from the comparison, the differences among the judges declines to a point of nonsignificance $(P>0.30)$.[2] In brief, the findings suggest that the judges tend toward a reasonable uniformity in the length of the penitentiary sentences they impose. The degree of uniformity, as will be shown by the case study analysis in the next chapter, is much greater than the statistical analysis implies.

The Effect of the Prosecutor on Sentence Variations

Critiques of the administration of criminal justice in the United States have accorded due recognition to the influence of the prosecuting attorney upon the deliberations of the sentencing judge. Summarizing the prevailing view of the prosecutor's role in the disposition of criminal cases, the writers of a leading American criminology textbook state:[3]

> The prosecutor is the most important person in the judicial system under present conditions. . . . The prosecutor determines whether a particular case shall be prosecuted. He determines whether a compromise shall be accepted, which generally means a plea of guilty to a lesser offence in return for a recommendation for mitigation of penalty. He is responsible for the organization and presentation of evidence before the court, and upon his efficiency in doing this the decision of the court depends. He is generally very influential in regard to the

---

[1] Appendix, Table 48.   [2] Appendix, Table 49.

[3] Sutherland and Cressey, *op. cit.*, p. 377.

disposition of cases, suggesting to the judge or jury the appropriate penalty. In fact, he is almost an absolute ruler of the judicial process.

We proceed, therefore, to test the hypothesis that differences among prosecutors, presumably in the skill or vigour with which they present their cases, affect the severity of the sentences imposed by the judge. A total of nineteen assistants to the District Attorney of the city of Philadelphia prosecuted the cases making up the research sample. Commonly, though not always, two assistant district attorneys each appearing in court on alternate weeks are assigned to a trial court for a term lasting about a month.

A comparison of the various prosecutors shows that they differ considerably in the proportions of the various types of penalties imposed upon the defendants in their respective case loads. The range of percentages of each type of penalty is as follows: penitentiary sentences, 18 to 42·9; prison sentences with minima of 3 to 11½ months, 10·3 to 43·1; non-prison sentences, 31·1 to 55·2 (P 0·001).[1]

Since these variations may be a function of differences in the sentencing practices of the judges before whom the cases are tried, the next step in the analysis is the comparison of the sentences of the different prosecutors in cases tried before the same judge. The case loads of seven of the judges are suitable for this purpose in that each of them includes two or more assistant district attorneys having enough cases for purposes of statistical analysis. In each test, the differences among the prosecutors in the proportions of the various types of penalties are not significant (P>0·70, 0·30, 0·50, 0·20, 0·10, 0·20, 0·30).[2]

Is there a tendency for the prosecutors to rank consistently high or low with each judge according to the relative severity of the sentences received by his defendants? Out of the six assistant district attorneys who prosecuted cases before two or more judges, two of them, "c" and "l", rank consistently high and one, "j", ranks consistently low. However, each of the other three assistant district attorneys, "h", "e", and "a", rank high before one judge but low before another.

Thus we conclude that *differences among prosecutors* do not have any significant effect upon variation in the severity of sentences.

---

[1] Appendix, Table 50.   [2] Appendix, Table 51.

Variations in Sentences according to the Plea of the Defendant

The belief is prevalent in legal circles that the defendant who pleads guilty thereby saving the state the expense of a trial receives a lighter punishment than the one who pleads not guilty and is subsequently found guilty. A comparison of cases involving guilty pleas with those involving not guilty pleas appears to refute this notion, a considerably greater percentage of the former receiving penitentiary sentences (29·9 : 20·2).[1]

It is doubtful, however, that judges show preference to offenders who have pleaded not guilty over those who have pleaded guilty. The fact is that the proportion of guilty pleas mounts directly with increases in the gravity of the offences and in the number of bills of indictment in the charge.[2] Pleas of guilty are entered in all of the 28 cases of homicide and in 63·4 per cent of narcotics cases; in 58·5 per cent of robbery cases charged in three or more bills of indictment but only in 29·3 per cent of robbery cases charged in one to two bills; in 76·1 per cent of burglary cases charged in three or more bills of indictment but only in 48·3 per cent of burglary cases charged in one or two bills. The association between the number of bills of indictment and the type of plea does not occur in larceny cases — the percentage of guilty pleas in cases involving three or more bills of indictment is virtually identical with that in cases involving fewer bills (48·6 : 47·7). The smallest proportion of guilty pleas, only 36·8 per cent, occurs in misdemeanour cases.

Upon controlling for differences between the plea categories in the gravity of the cases we find that in 7 out of 10 statistical tests the differences in sentences according to plea are statistically non-significant.[3] In fact, there is near equality between the two plea categories in the proportional distribution of the various types of penalties within the following offence categories: felonious crimes against the person (P = 1·0), robbery charged in one to two bills of indictment (P>0·90), and burglary charged in one to two bills of indictment (P>0·90).[4]

The differences are somewhat greater but still not significant in cases of narcotic drug violations charged in two or more bills (P>0·50), burglary charged in three or more bills (P>0·10)

---

[1] Appendix, Table 52.   [2] Appendix, Table 53.
[3] Appendix, Table 54.   [4] Appendix, Table 54.

larceny charged in three or more bills ($P > 0.05$) and misdemeanours ($P > 0.05$). The differences are significant, however, in cases of robbery charged in three or more bills of indictment ($0.05 > P > 0.02$) and in narcotics violations charged in one bill of indictment ($0.05 > P > 0.02$). In each of these comparisons except that for the cases of narcotic drug violations charged in two or more bills of indictment the defendants who plead guilty receive harsher sentences.[1]

The most reasonable explanation for this surprising grant of leniency to offenders who plead not guilty is that the tendency of defence counsels to plead their more serious cases guilty in the hope of earning judicial clemency for their clients operates unnoticed in the foregoing statistical experiments. This notion finds support in the observation that defendants charged with larceny or burglary in three or more bills of indictment who plead guilty have a more serious history of recidivism than those who plead not guilty. In larceny the percentages of guilty and not guilty pleas accompanied by one or more prior felony convictions are 64.7 and 47.2, respectively; and in burglary, 65.5 and 48.8. It is also likely, but not demonstrable by our data, that the cases with guilty pleas contain a higher percentage of crimes of a more aggravated nature than the cases with not guilty pleas.

Only in cases of larceny charged in one to two bills, is it clear that the accused accrues any benefit by a plea of guilty; only 13.2 per cent of the defendants who plead guilty compared with 20 per cent of those who plead not guilty receive penitentiary sentences. This difference in minor offences against property may reflect the mitigating effect of the offer to make restitution which is more likely to accompany a guilty plea than a not guilty plea.

To recapitulate, the results suggest that defence attorneys place reliance upon the belief that the court will be disposed to react more leniently toward convicted defendants who have pleaded guilty than toward those who have pleaded not guilty. The confidence of the attorney is understandable in view of the fact that in explaining or justifying his sentences, the judge frequently states how much worse the sentence could have been if he had not taken into consideration one or another mitigating circumstance, usually the co-operation of the defendant with the police or the court.[2] The data show conclusively, however, that the confidence of the attorney is misplaced, that the belief upon which it rests is delusive.

---

[1] *Ibid.*   [2] See Chapter VII.

Summary

In this chapter we have examined the effect of certain factors in the administration of justice — the judge, the prosecutor, and the plea of the defendant — upon the severity of the sentences received by offenders. Neither individual differences among the prosecutors nor differences in the plea appreciably affect variation in the penalties. The effect of individual differences among the judges tends to be most pronounced in cases of intermediate gravity, declining as the cases approach the polarities of the petty or grave offence. There is no evidence, however, of undue disparity among the judges in the length of the penitentiary sentences imposed.

VII

CASE STUDIES IN SENTENCING

STATISTICAL analysis possesses the virtue of presenting in broad outline the network of factors producing variations in penalties for crimes. But like a skeleton which, to be sure, discloses inferentially a great deal about the nature of the living organism, it lacks breath and pulse. It does not provide any direct insight into the world of meanings — the penal philosophies, the theories of crime causation, the conceptions of human nature — by which the judges rationalize their sentences. The quality of the wholeness of each case is of necessity sacrificed in statistical analysis — a detailed picture of the specific behaviour constituting the criminal charge; the claims concerning the offender's intent, mental state at time of the crime, or status adduced in mitigation or aggravation of the penalty, filter through the statistical sieve.

Our general objective in this chapter is to complement the statistical analysis by the intensive exploration of individual cases. Our specific aims are as follows: to perceive the cases in their wholeness, to capture something of the drama of the sentencing process, to note the judges' expression of their penal philosophies, and to verify the results of the statistical analysis.

The data derive from the *Notes of Testimony*, a verbatim reproduction of the trial proceedings recorded by the court stenographer. The information in each case will consist of the offender's age, sex, race; a statement of the act(s) constituting the offence; the offender's prior criminal record; the plea; the sentence; and whatever comment by the judge or exchange between him and the defendant, assistant district attorney, defence counsel, or victim that relates to the imposition of the sentence.

The thirty cases to be analysed are a random sample drawn from those cases for which the *Notes of Testimony* were at the time of the research transcribed and filed in the office of the Clerk of the Quarter Sessions Court. They are grouped for purposes of analysis into the following five categories:

A. Habitual offenders whose criminality poses a grave threat to the public safety.

B. Offenders who have accidentally committed a serious crime of violence during the commission of a lesser crime.

C. Chronic offenders or parole violators convicted of crimes of intermediate gravity.

D. Occasional or first offenders charged with crimes of intermediate gravity.

E. Offenders convicted of minor crimes (misdemeanours) whose prior records reveal no serious pattern of transgression.

A. Habitual Offenders whose Criminality Poses a Grave Threat to Public Safety

A–1

Defendant: male, Negro, age 26. *Charge:* 2 bills of indictment for aggravated robbery and 1 for conspiracy. *Prior Criminal Record:* 2 felony convictions. *Plea:* guilty. *Sentence:* on the indictments for aggravated robbery, two terms of 5 to 10 years to run consecutively (10 to 20 years); sentence suspended for conspiracy. *Judge:* N.

The defendant and an accomplice were convicted of twice luring victims from a barroom whereupon they beat and robbed them. The amounts taken were $40 in one case and $50 in the other. The defendant, a parole violator with 7 years' back time from a sentence of 3 to 10 years for previous convictions of armed robbery and larceny pleaded guilty. The comment of the court was brief: "These are crimes of violence and must be dealt with severely. I see no other way out."

A–2

Defendant: male, white, age 23. *Charge:* 1 indictment for robbery, 1 indictment for burglary, 15 indictments for larcenies. *Prior Criminal Record:* 3 arrests, no convictions. *Sentence:* 5 to 20 years — 3 to 10 years for robbery and 2 to 10 years for burglary, the two terms to run consecutively; sentence suspended on the other bills of indictment. *Judge:* G.

The defendant was the ring leader of a group of young criminals who committed a series of larcenies, a burglary, and one robbery (not aggravated robbery).

The court elicited from the defendant that his father had deserted him and his mother when he was very young. The mother was called to testify in her son's behalf. She turned out to be an unfavourable witness for the defence, stating that her son could not get along with other members of the family at home, that ". . . the world owed him a living".

The Court: "If it weren't for what the officers have said and the impression you have made upon me by the way in which you appeared to tell the truth I would give you a very substantial sentence and you would spend the rest of your life in prison."

A–3

Defendant: male, white, age 24. *Charge:* 1 indictment for robbery, 1 indictment for aggravated assault and battery. *Prior Criminal Record:* 3 felony convictions. *Plea:* not guilty. *Sentence:* 5 to 20 years. *Judge:* B.

The defendant severely beat a man in a barroom fight and then left town. He returned a few weeks later and with an accomplice robbed a loan office of $1,245.

The court noting that the defendant did not use a gun in the robbery, stated: ". . . but he pretended to have a gun and struck the same terror in the mind of that woman (the victim)."

". . . He is vicious. That fellow needs to be tamed."

The court determined that the defendant was married and the father of a two-year-old child to whose support he was not contributing.

The judge threatened to impose a sentence of 7 to 20 years, 2 to 5[1] of which was for the aggravated assault and battery but modified it to 5 to 20 years on the plea of the defence counsel that the defendant had been co-operative with the police and the court.

A–4

Defendant: male, Negro, age 35. *Charge:* aggravated robbery (at gun point), assault to kill, and violation of the fire arms act. *Verdict:* guilty of aggravated robbery. *Prior Criminal Record:* 2 felony

---

[1] Two to five years is not a legal sentence for aggravated assault and battery. The maximum for this offence allowed by statute in Pennsylvania is three years.

convictions, 1 misdemeanour conviction. *Plea:* guilty. *Sentence:* 5 to 20 years. *Judge:* C.

The defendant armed with a gun held up a real estate office taking $3. The victim pursued the robber with a revolver wounding him in both legs.

The judge elicited from the defendant that he was separated from his wife, received a 50 per cent disability pension from the government for military service, and had a neurosis while in the service.

The defence counsel, assigned to represent the defendant by the *Voluntary Defender* requested the court, "... not to set an arbitrarily high minimum, that the parole board will have a much better opportunity to observe this defendant and size him up, so that I would ask Your Honour not to foreclose his opportunity for parole for a long period of time."

The Court: "Well this is the kind of crime in which the sentence ought to be, normally, 10 to 20 years. Now I will cut his minimum down only because he was shot in both legs, and I am giving him credit for having got part of his punishment that way, and that is the only reason I am cutting it."

A–5

Defendant: male, Negro, age 32. *Charge:* 2 indictments for the sale of narcotic drugs. *Prior Criminal Record:* 2 convictions of narcotic drug violations, 1 of burglary. *Plea:* not guilty. *Sentence:* 2 terms of 2 to 5 years, each, to run consecutively (4 to 10 years) and a fine of $4,000. *Judge:* M.

The defendant was convicted of selling narcotic drugs to two police operatives. He admitted that he was convicted in 1954 for the possession and use of drugs.

No comment was made by the court on the reason for imposing this particular sentence. It will be recalled, however, that the law restricts the discretion of the judge in sentencing narcotics offenders by requiring that a penitentiary sentence has a minimum term of at least two years.

Commentary

The attitudes expressed by the judges toward offenders whom neither the fear of imprisonment nor the previous experience of imprisonment has deterred from repeated miscreancy are strongly retributive. The rather long terms of imprisonment meted out in these cases suggest that the primary objective sought is the isolation of the offender from society. Interestingly, in three of the four robbery cases (A–2, A–3, and A–4), each judge threatened a heavier sentence than the one imposed, and the amount of the sentence threatened differs in all three cases; yet the sentences are the same (5 to 20 years). It is unlikely that any of the judges had the intention of imposing a sentence other than the one pronounced. Case A–2 illustrates this point. The judge could not actually impose the threatened sentence of life imprisonment because the defendant had not committed a capital offence and his prior criminal record did not meet the criterion for a life sentence under the habitual offender law. The only way the judge could have imposed what is in effect a life sentence would be to pronounce consecutive sentences for each of the 17 bills of indictment on which the defendant was convicted.

The fact that the defendant in Case A–1 received double the minimum term in any of the other robbery cases is not in itself an indication that the sentencing judge is unduly severe but, rather, of the fact that the defendant was a parole violator, the 7 years of the unexpired term of a previous sentence serving to aggravate the penalty. Case A–5 involves a narcotics peddler convicted of his third offence. Under the law he was liable to a penalty with a minimum term of 10 years and a maximum term of 30 years on each bill. Viewed in this light, the penalty imposed, 2 terms of 2 to 5 years to run consecutively, is rather mild.

B. Offenders who have accidentally Committed a Serious Crime of Violence during the Commission of a Lesser Crime

B–1

Defendant: male, Negro, age 16. *Charge:* murder in the second degree. *Prior Criminal Record:* none. *Plea:* guilty. *Judge:* G.

The defendant while fleeing a police chase in a stolen car struck and killed a pedestrian.

The Court: "Young man, the penalty for your offence is not less than 10 and no more than 20 years in the Eastern State Penitentiary, but we . . . have a provision for confining you to an institution where you would receive valuable training at the Industrial School for Boys at Whitehill.

"And, if you are sent there as I intend to send you, you are committed without a fixed term."

The court continued, saying that if the defendant's attitude and conduct would warrant, there is a likelihood that within a "reasonable and proper" time, he could gain freedom.

The assistant district attorney advised the judge that the sentence he proposed was illegal, that for a conviction of murder, the place of confinement must be the Eastern State Penitentiary. The sentence was accordingly changed to 6 to 12 years in the Eastern State Penitentiary.

B–2

Defendant: male, Negro, age 26. *Charge:* voluntary manslaughter. *Prior Criminal Record:* 2 felony convictions and 2 misdemeanour convictions. *Plea:* not guilty. *Sentence:* 4 to 12 years. *Judge:* O.

The victim, in an intoxicated state, walked onto the street from his house where he became involved in an altercation with the defendant who claimed that the victim had made advances to his wife. The defendant beat the victim to death kicking him with such force that internal organs were ruptured.

The Court: "I have considered all the evidence and I have taken into consideration the law that has been offered before me and have concluded that this was not a killing in self defence. It was rather a killing without malice but committed under the immediate influence of sudden passion and hot blood induced by adequate legal provocation as a result of which the defendant's reason was disturbed or obstructed and he acted rashly without deliberation. I therefore adjudge him guilty of voluntary manslaughter. What about his past?

"As far as sentence is concerned I will take into consideration that considerable time has been saved by the defendant pleading guilty as he has and I will not subject him to punishment that would ordinarily be imposed in a case of voluntary manslaughter. . . . A fair sentence in this case would be more than could be properly imposed on voluntary manslaughter."

After the averment of the defendant's prior criminal record, the court stated: "I should really sentence you more than I had

F

originally intended in view of your record but I will give you a sentence that I had originally intended to give you in view of your guilty plea. What do you have to say, Mr. District Attorney?"

Assistant District Attorney: "I go along with Your Honour's thought."

Defence Counsel: "Before Your Honour imposes sentence I would just like to add that the death was caused by a single blow because of an altercation in which the two men were participating. There was no weapon and I think that should be given serious consideration in the imposition of sentence."

The Court: "He is lucky he isn't here for murder in the second degree. The maximum sentence would be 6 to 12 years (for voluntary manslaughter). I will cut the minimum down. I want some control over him. I will sentence him to 4 to 12 years. I am cutting two years off."

Commentary

In each of these cases death was accidentally inflicted in the course of a relatively minor offence. Had the sixteen-year-old defendant in B–1 not struck a pedestrian while driving the vehicle or if he had only injured the victim, his case would have come before the juvenile court. Likewise had the victim in B–2 not died of his injuries, the charge against the defendant would have been aggravated assault and battery, a misdemeanour.

Homicide, however, is regarded by tradition as so grave that for the court to fail to impose a heavy penalty would defeat the expectations of the public. Accordingly the sentences imposed reflect the retributive theory of punishment implicit in the law. Even advocates of a more conservative policy in the administration of criminal justice might agree that a disposition tailored in terms of rehabilitative goals would have been more desirable than a penitentiary sentence in the case of the sixteen-year-old boy. Although the sentencing judge was apparently in accord with this view, the retributive requirement of the law precluded his utilization of the more treatment oriented type of disposition.

C. Chronic Offenders or Parole Violators Convicted of Crimes of Intermediate Gravity

C–1

Defendant: male, Negro, age 41. *Charge:* 1 indictment of burglary and 1 indictment for aggravated assault and battery. *Prior Criminal Record:* 4 prior felony convictions. *Plea:* not guilty. *Sentence:* for burglary, 2 to 5 years; sentence suspended for aggravated assault and battery. *Judge:* L.

The defendant broke into a house stealing clothes and household goods worth $300. He also slashed with a knife the woman with whom he lived.

The defence counsel stated that the defendant was employed as a truck driver's helper and had been living with the prosecutrix on the aggravated assault and battery charge for four years.

No comment was made by the court on the sentence.

C–2

Defendant: male, Negro, age 32. *Charge:* 1 indictment for burglary. *Prior Criminal Record:* 5 felony convictions. *Plea:* not guilty. *Sentence:* 1½ to 3 years. *Judge:* G.

The defendant was convicted of entering a room in a hotel and removing a radio from the wall. The assistant district attorney stated: "This man has a very substantial record as you can see."

No comment was made by the sentencing judge.

C–3

Defendant: male, white, age 24. *Charge:* 1 indictment for burglary, 4 indictments for forgery. *Prior Criminal Record:* 1 felony conviction (burglary). *Sentence:* 1 to 3 years in the Eastern State Penitentiary on the burglary indictment; sentence suspended on the forgery indictments. *Judge:* C.

The defendant broke into a store, stole a television set and some checks. An accomplice forged the checks and cashed them.

The court elicited from the defendant that he was single, both of his parents were dead, that he was brought up by various relatives, and that he was a truck driver.

The prior conviction of burglary resulting in a sentence of 1 to 2 years was averred.

The Court: "Well, each time the sentence gets heavier, you know. 1 to 3 years in the Eastern Penitentiary."

C–4

Defendant: male, white, age 25. *Charge:* 1 indictment for burglary of auto, 1 for unlawfully resisting an officer making an arrest, and 2 for receiving stolen goods. The defendant was found guilty of burglary of auto and receiving stolen goods. *Prior Criminal Record:* 1 conviction of burglary. The defendant was on parole at the time of this offence. *Plea:* guilty. *Sentence:* 1 to 3 years. *Judge:* B.

The defendant was arrested by an off-duty policeman while rummaging through the policeman's automobile. The defendant broke away and was recaptured. Found in his room were numerous pawn tickets and articles taken from burglarized vehicles.

The court averred the prior criminal record of the defendant, noting also that he had served in the army.

The Court: "We can't do much about this fellow. He is on probation and it doesn't mean anything to him. He is not living at home, and he has absolutely no anchor.

"You are not a vicious fellow at all. But you have a record. By the time you are forty you will have nothing but crime on your record. I will make it 1 to 3 years in County Prison."

Defence Counsel: "It may be difficult for him to get parole."

The Court: "I can't help that. If it is difficult he made it difficult."

C–5

Defendant: male, white, age 37. *Charge:* 1 indictment for burglary. *Prior Criminal Record:* 2 felony convictions, 3 misdemeanour convictions. *Plea:* guilty. *Sentence:* 1 to 3 years. *Judge:* F.

The defendant broke into the cellar window of a residence and took $120 from the kitchen table.

The judge interrogated the defendant concerning his background and brought out that he had served two enlistments in the army, receiving an honourable discharge. The court also took note of the defendant's prior criminal record.

The defence counsel attested that the defendant had been co-operative with the police, that "liquor seems to be his trouble".

The Court: "Oh there is probably some liquor involved but he was sentenced in 1953 to 1 to 3 years and his maximum was up January 3rd, 1956. So it wasn't too long after that, about seven months, that he was back inside of a dwelling house.

"That is the difficulty here: he doesn't seem to learn a lesson."

C–6

Defendant: male, Negro, age 18. *Charge:* 1 indictment for burglary, 1 indictment for conspiracy. *Prior Criminal Record:* 1 felony conviction. *Plea:* not guilty. *Sentence:* indeterminate to the State Industrial School. *Judge:* O.

The defendant and an accomplice were caught by the police at 2 a.m. removing three automobile radiators, one battery, and one fire extinguisher from a building.

The Court: "I think Camp Hill (the State Industrial School) would be a better place for M—— (the defendant)."

The defendant's accomplice, age 22, was sentenced to the County Prison for 11½ to 23 months.

C–7

Defendant: male, Negro, age 41. *Charge:* burglary of a vehicle. *Prior Criminal Record:* 3 felony convictions, 10 misdemeanour convictions. *Plea:* not guilty. *Sentence:* 6 to 23 months. *Judge:* O.

The defendant was convicted of stealing a valise containing medical supplies from a physician's automobile. The defendant denied the theft, claiming he found the valise in a trash pile.

Prior to imposing sentence, the Court reviewed the defendant's lengthy prior criminal record.

Defence Counsel: "All I can say, sir, when you reduce it, it becomes two convictions of any importance. The rest of the stuff is like a vagabond and common nuisance."

The Court: "Look at the story he tried to put across today. He tried to convince me that he found it in a trash can. (To the defendant) Don't you have any respect for the Bible?"

Defendant: "Yes, I do."

The Court: "In what way?"

Defendant: "I believe in the Bible."

The Court: "You put your hand on the Bible and you try to

tell me a story like that saying you found this. Where is your home?"

Defendant: "Tallahassee, Florida."

The Court: "6 to 23 months in County Prison."

Commentary

In these cases, all of which involve convictions of burglary committed by recidivists, the comment of the judges, where expressed, reflects impatience but not outrage with the incorrigibility of the offender. The import of the sentences expressed in the comment of the judges is to intimidate the defendant by affording him a stern lesson. It is noteworthy that Case C–1 containing an additional indictment for aggravated assault and battery received the heaviest penalty and Case C–2 revealing a pattern of chronic recidivism and on parole when convicted received the next heaviest penalty. The sentence in C–7 appears to be relatively mild compared to those imposed in the other cases.

D. Occasional or First Offenders Charged with Crimes of Intermediate Gravity

D–1

Defendant: male, Negro, age 38. *Charge:* 1 indictment for aggravated assault and battery, 1 indictment for carrying concealed deadly weapons. *Prior Criminal Record:* 11 misdemeanour convictions. *Plea:* not guilty. *Sentence:* 1½ to 3 years. *Judge:* O.

The defendant was convicted of stabbing the complainant in the back without provocation.

The Court: "You have a record, you come from North Carolina."

Defendant: "Yes."

The Court: "You did time in Davidson, North Carolina and Winston-Salem, North Carolina and Greensboro, North Carolina."

The defence counsel point out that most of the defendant's prior arrests were before 1944. Since then the defendant had had only two arrests on minor charges.

The Court: "Eighteen months to 3 years."

Defence Counsel: "Would Your Honour hear me another minute in mitigation? I want his mother to stand up and identify the mother in court in order that Your Honour would know that she is here interested in him."

The Court: "Do you want the mother to testify?"

Defence Counsel: "No."

The Court: "Eighteen months to 3 years in County Prison."

D-2

Defendant: female, Negro, age 21. *Charge:* 1 indictment for aggravated robbery, 1 indictment for playfully and wantonly pointing a gun, 1 for conspiracy, and 3 for carrying concealed deadly weapons. *Verdict:* guilty of robbery. *Prior Criminal Record:* none. *Plea:* not guilty. *Sentence:* indeterminate to the Women's Reformatory. *Judge:* G.

The defendant was convicted of driving the getaway car in an armed robbery.

She was married and the mother of three children.

The court made no comment on the sentence.

D-3

Defendant: male, Negro, age 21. *Charge:* statutory rape. *Prior Criminal Record:* 1 indeterminate commitment to the Youth Reformatory for 3 years. *Plea:* not guilty. *Sentence:* 1 to 3 years in the penitentiary. *Judge:* G.

The defendant had sexual intercourse with a female aged fifteen.

The court averred a prior commitment to the Youth Reformatory for the same offence.

The court made no comment on the sentence.

Two weeks later the sentence was vacated and reduced to 11½ to 23 months in the County Prison.

D-4

Defendant: female, Negro, age 31. *Charge:* the possession and use of narcotic drugs. *Prior Criminal Record:* none. *Plea:* not guilty. *Sentence:* 6 to 12 months. *Judge:* M.

Police detectives entered the defendant's room and found articles used by drug addicts and evidences of heroin. The defendant was examined by the police physician whose diagnosis was positive for the use of drugs.

There was no comment by the court regarding the sentence.

D–5

Defendant: male, white, age 18. *Charge:* 3 indictments for burglary. *Prior Criminal Record:* 1 conviction for burglary as a juvenile. *Plea:* guilty. *Sentence:* 5 years' probation. *Judge:* C.

The defendant and an accomplice committed a series of burglaries in a neighbouring county and locally. The defendant enlisted in the navy. After 5 months he was apprehended by the police, discharged from the navy, convicted in the neighbouring jurisdiction, and sentenced to a term of 11½ to 23 months in the County Prison. Upon release from prison, he was arrested on a warrant issued by the local court for the crimes committed in this jurisdiction.

The court ascertained that the defendant's record since the burglary escapade had been good. He had not been in trouble while in the navy. The defendant's father was present.

The Court: "How old are you?"

Defendant: "Nineteen, sir."

The Court: "It seems to me the penalties up there were rather light."

Defence Counsel: "Well I think if Your Honour pleases, their ages had something to do with it. I guess they were both closer to eighteen at that time; they were first offenders at that time."

The Court: "I guess it would be better for me to keep a long string on them for a good while rather than send them to jail. That's what I'll do. Five years probation. It's a long string."

D–6

Defendant: male, Negro, age 33. *Charge:* aggravated assault and battery. *Prior Criminal Record:* 1 conviction of felony. *Plea:* guilty. *Sentence:* 30 days to 23 months in the County Prison. *Judge:* O.

The defendant nicked his wife with a knife during an argument.

The court noted that the defendant's prior criminal record was not serious and that the defendant and his wife had four children.

The Court: (addressing the defendant's wife) "How much time do you want me to give him? How long do you want me to keep him away from you?"

Defendant's Wife: Judge, Your Honour, I would like you to give him 30 days on parole."

The Court: "Thirty days on parole?"

Defendant's Wife: "On probation."

The Court: "Suppose I send him to jail for you? Could you get along without him?"

Defendant's Wife: "I got so many little children to support."

The Court: "Suppose he stabbed you and you died? Who would support the children? He has got to be punished. He has got to know he can't use a knife."

The judge then threatened imprisonment for one year but relented and made the sentence 30 days to 23 months.

D-7

Defendant: male, white, age 39. *Charge:* 2 indictments for larceny. *Prior Criminal Record:* 1 misdemeanour conviction. *Plea:* guilty. *Sentence:* 2 years probation and restitution. *Judge:* F.

The defendant stole plumbing fittings worth $530 from building operations. The court determined that a portion of the stolen goods had already been returned and that more was recoverable; also that the defendant was divorced and contributed to the support of a thirteen-year-old daughter.

The court averred one prior conviction for lottery-making.

The Court: "How long have you been in jail?"

Court Clerk: "Thirty days."

The Court: "How would you like to stay there for a good while?"

Defendant: "I wouldn't like it."

The Court: "Do you think we ought to give him an opportunity?"

Assistant District Attorney: "I think so."

D-8

Defendant: male, Negro, age 19. *Charge:* burglary of auto. *Prior Criminal Record:* 1 juvenile conviction. *Plea:* guilty. *Sentence:* 2 to 23 months in County Prison. *Judge:* C.

The police apprehended the defendant after he broke the rear window of a motor vehicle and took two boxes of aluminium cookware, valued at $50 each.

Defence Counsel: "A——, speak up loud and face the judge. How old are you?"

Defendant: "Nineteen."

Defence Counsel: "Are you married or single?"

Defendant: "Single."

Defence Counsel: "With whom do you live?"

Defendant: "My mother."

Defence Counsel: "What do you do?"

Defendant: "I hustle, sell vegetables."

Defence Counsel: "Why did you do this?"

Defendant: "I was walking up the street at the time and I saw it there, and at the time I needed a little money, my money was ——."

Defence Counsel: "Have you been in trouble before?"

Defendant: "I served three months in the House of Correction, a fight."

The Court: "What was that?"

Defendant: "Disorderly conduct, fighting."

The Court: "Who were you fighting?"

Defendant: "A police officer."

The Court: "How old were you at that time?"

Defendant: "Seventeen."

The Court: "Is that all the trouble?"

Defendant: "Yes sir."

The Court: "Is that the first one you had broken into?"

Defendant: "Yes sir."

The Court: "Are you sure of that?"

Defendant: "Yes sir. I had usually been working. See, I have a job now. When I do get out I have a job."

The Court: "Well it's a first offence, but I think you have got to spend some time for this."

Defendant: "Sir, I have decided if you give me a break, I'd like to join the service."

The Court: "I don't think they'll take you, sorry."

Defendant: "I have a job now to go back to."

The Court: "I won't keep you there, but you have to do a little bit. Two to 23 months in the County Prison."[1]

D–9

Defendant: male, Negro, age 24. *Charge:* 2 indictments for burglary. *Prior Criminal Record:* none. *Plea:* guilty. *Sentence:* 34 days to 23 months and probation for two years. *Judge:* N.

[1] Since the defendant had spent over 50 days in jail awaiting trial his release on a bench parole was imminent.

The defendant stole a radio and a suit from the apartment of a friend. The defence counsel stated that the defendant had no prior criminal record. In testimony elicited by the defence counsel, the defendant stated that he is twenty-four years of age, married, and separated from his wife and four small children.

The Court: "Are you supporting them (the children)?"

Defendant: "Yes."

The Court: "What type of work do you do?"

Defendant: "Mostly anything."

The Court: "How come you did this?"

Defendant: "Like I said, Your Honour, I was drinking and I needed some money."

The Court: "If you have three or four kids, why do you spend money on drink?"

There was no response to this question. The court then determined that the stolen property had been returned to its owner.

The Court: "How long has he been in prison?"

Defence Counsel: "Thirty-four days."

The Court: "Well that might be sufficient. What do you think Mr. Assistant District Attorney?"

Assistant District Attorney: "I think so."

The Court: "How do you feel about it Mr. D—— (the victim)?"

Mr. D——: "It's up to the Court."

The Court: "I will put it this way: on the burglary charge I will make it 34 days to 23 months. On the other bill I will make it a probationary period of 2 years after this so that we can watch him if he gets in trouble."

Commentary

The sentences for these cases appear to be sensible in terms of the legal criteria for sentencing. The penalty imposed in the case of the defendant who stabbed his victim in the back (D–1) is notably heavier than the others in this category and is exceeded only by one case, also involving violence, in the preceding category of cases (C–1). The penalty for the aggravated assault and battery in Case D–6 is mild because it occurred incident to a family spat, no consequential injury resulting. The probation granted the burglar in Case D–5 might appear to be lenient considering the number of bills of indictment charged. The defendant, however, had just completed a fairly substantial prison sentence in a neighbouring county for one of the series of offences the others of which he was tried for in this case. The sentences in the other property cases — D–7, D–8, and D–9 — are all rather mild.

The criminal act in each of the remaining cases is a minor variant of the offence charged. Case D–2, the female robber, was only an accessary; Case D–3, the rapist, was guilty only of statutory rape; Case D–4, was only a user of narcotics. The sentence imposed in each of these cases therefore is understandably relatively mild compared to the sentences generally imposed for such offences.

E. OFFENDERS CONVICTED OF MINOR CRIMES WHOSE PRIOR RECORDS REVEAL NO SERIOUS CRIMINAL CAREER

E–1

Defendant: male, Negro, age 22. *Charge:* solicitation for prostitution. *Prior Criminal Record:* 1 felony conviction and 5 misdemeanour convictions. *Sentence:* 12 months. *Judge:* M.

The defendant pandered among sailors in a barroom.

The court averred the defendant's prior criminal record, including a conviction for desertion from the armed forces and four convictions for pandering.

The court did not comment on the sentence.

E–2

Defendant: male, Negro, age 30. *Charge:* assault and battery. *Prior Criminal Record:* 1 felony conviction and 2 misdemeanour convictions (all assaults). *Plea:* guilty. *Sentence:* 2 years (concurrent with a prison sentence now being served). *Judge:* O.

The defendant was brought from prison where he was serving time for a prior conviction to stand trial for beating his common law wife. The court averred a prior conviction for aggravated assault and battery with a razor on another woman.

The court made no comment on the sentence.

The penalty is in effect a suspended sentence inasmuch as it runs concurrently with the remainder of the time on the sentence for the prior conviction.

E–3

Defendant: male, Negro, age 26. *Charge:* operating a motor vehicle without the consent of the owner, assault and battery, resisting arrest, unlawfully failing to stop and render assistance after an accident, and carrying concealed deadly weapons. *Prior Criminal Record:* 2 prior felony convictions. *Plea:* guilty. *Sentence:* 3 years probation for operating a motor vehicle without the consent of the owner; sentence suspended on the other indictments. *Judge:* C.

The defendant took an automobile, not his own, and while driving scraped a parked vehicle. Police detectives stopped him for questioning whereupon he threw the car into reverse gear and gunned the motor, throwing the detectives to the ground. They were uninjured. The detectives caught up with the defendant and subdued him after a struggle. On the way to the police station, the defendant hit a detective, broke out of the police car, and fled. The defendant was recaptured. The defendant denied hitting the detective stating he fled because he was beaten. The defendant is married, living with his wife, has one child, is employed, and is on probation for a previous offence.

The Court: "Why did you do this when you were still on probation?"

Defendant: "I don't know Your Honour. It was a pretty dumb trick, wasn't it?"

The Court: "Yes sir, I guess it was. How long has he been in now?"

Court Clerk: "Thirty-one days."

The Court: "He has been in thirty-one days. Well the advice here (a neuropsychiatric examination) is to put you on probation again. I really shouldn't, and yet I will. Maybe the fellow that does such dumb tricks as you can be kept straight if he knows he is going to get into real trouble if he does it anymore. How much damage was done to that car? The officers weren't hurt, were they?"

Assistant District Attorney: "No sir, fortunately."

Defence Counsel: "And the damage to the car was just a scratch."

E–4

Defendant: male, white, age 63. *Charge:* Larceny. *Prior Criminal Record:* 9 misdemeanour convictions. *Plea:* guilty. *Sentence:* 3 to 12 months. *Judge:* O.

The defendant broke a parking meter and stole coins from it.

The Court: "Wouldn't you be better off to stay in jail during the cold weather?"

Defendant: "I would, yes sir, but not too long."

The Court: "How long has he been in jail?"

Assistant District Attorney: "Eighty-five days."

The Court: "When do you think the weather will be warm enough?"

Defendant: "May 1st."

The Court: "Three months to 1 year. We will see that you get out on May 1st."

E–6

Defendant: male, white, age 19. *Charge:* contributing to the delinquency of a minor. *Prior Criminal Record:* none. *Sentence:* 19 days to 23 months. *Judge:* O.

The defendant kept a girl under sixteen years of age in his apartment overnight.

The Court: "Has he ever been in trouble before?"

Defence Counsel: "No he hasn't. He hasn't been working. This young lady came in to the apartment and spent the night with him. She told him she was much older than she really was."

The Court: "How long has he been in jail?"

Court Clerk: "Nineteen days."

The Court: "Nineteen days to 23 months."

E–7

Defendant: male, race not given, age 61. *Charge:* the possession of untaxed liquor. *Prior Criminal Record:* No record in the file. *Plea:* guilty. *Sentence:* $100 or 30 days. *Judge:* O.

The defendant was arrested in the street in possession of one pint of untaxed liquor.

The Court: "How old is he?"

Defence Counsel: "He is sixty-one years of age. He is a widower and gets a pension from World War I and he served in the army and received an honourable discharge."

The Court: "He is a drunk and he drinks this kind of stuff that will satisfy his desires for drink. How long has he been in jail?"

Assistant District Attorney: "Twenty-three days."

The Court: "You have to stay another seven days. 30 days or $100 fine.

E–8

Defendant: male, Negro, age 25. *Charge:* illegal possession of fire arms. *Prior Criminal Record:* none. *Plea:* guilty. *Sentence:* 67 days to 12 months. *Judge:* M.

A police officer stopped the defendant while driving a motor vehicle and found a ·25 calibre pistol under the car seat. The defendant at the trial admitted ownership of the weapon.

Sentence followed with no comment.

Commentary

These minor cases were disposed of rather routinely, the judges less frequently than in more serious cases interjecting justifications or explanations of their sentences. Six out of the seven defendants in Class E have prior records of little consequence. All were convicted of minor crimes, and with one exception the sentences are of negligible weight. The disposition in the case of E–1 the panderer, is quite severe relative to the other sentences. The defendant in E–1, however, has a record of repeated commission of this offence. The sentence imposed in E–2, is in effect a suspended sentence inasmuch as it runs concurrently with the remainder of a prison sentence for a prior conviction. In the case of E–4, the sentence is hardly punitive, but rather an extension of the hospitality of the county during the cold winter weather!

SUMMARY

In general, the views expressed by the court are moralistic, reflecting the traditional view of criminal behaviour as a product of free will. The penal theories implicit in the judicial comment are an admixture of the retributive, the deterrent, and the rehabilitative. In cases of serious offences committed by offenders on whom the threat or the experience of imprisonment has had no restraining effect, the inclination of the judges is to isolate the offender from society for a long period of time. The attitude of the judges in the cases of homicide is essentially retributive. In cases of intermediate gravity committed by recidivists, the correctional goal implicit in the judicial comment is primarily deterrent. As the cases become less serious with regard to the gravity of the offence and the past record of the offender, the goal of rehabilitation is more evident. But whether the sentence embodies rehabilitative or punitive goals, it is not based on an estimate of the social or psychological condition of the offender but rather on the legal character of the case.

The specific reasons given by the judges for the mitigation of the sentence do not bear any consistent relationship to variation in penalties. We note, for example that the judges frequently set forth the co-operation of the defendant with the police or court as a factor in mitigation of the penalty. Yet, pleas of guilty which certainly signify a willingness to co-operate with the court are not rewarded by sentences of lesser severity than pleas of not guilty. We note also that in the two instances where the defendants were decidedly unco-operative with the arresting police officers (C–4 and E–3), the sentences are not heavier than those of other cases of similar gravity. In fact, throughout the cases of the study, the additional charge of resisting arrest does not appear to aggravate the sentence.

The data contradict the "bargain theory" of criminal justice, namely that the prosecutor will settle for a conviction of a less serious offence than that warranted by the criminal act in exchange for a plea of guilty. In each of the cases reviewed except perhaps one[1] the criminal act averred clearly lies within the purview of the offence charged.

Finally, the results of the case study analysis thoroughly corroborate the results of the statistical analysis. The variation in sentences within each category of cases and between adjoining categories of cases follows rather closely the differentiation of the cases according to the legal criteria derived from the statistical analysis. Indeed, it would be difficult to say that any of the sentences is unduly out of line with the others. The fact that the thirty cases derive from the case loads of nine different judges suggests how closely alike the judges are with respect to their scales of penal values.

---

[1] E–3 convicted of operating a motor vehicle without the consent of the owner, a misdemeanour, might just as well have been charged with larceny, a felony.

VIII

SUMMARY AND CONCLUSIONS

THE dearth of systematic analysis of the judicial process has forced upon students of jurisprudence and criminology the necessity of improvising a social psychology of the administration of justice. Incongruously, current theories of human motivation having wide application to the explanation of criminal behaviour are adapted to explain the official reaction to criminal behaviour. These assert that non-rational impulses such as blindly operating cultural forces or prejudice or unconscious psychological needs largely determine the judicial decision.

One of the major conclusions we have drawn is that sociolegal factors—statutory law, common law, common and legal conventions—impose sharp restrictions on judicial behaviour. These are the criteria by which the judges sentence and they are purposively applied in determining the relative seriousness of the cases.

The primary factor affecting variation in the severity of the sentences is the offence. The rank order of the various offences according to the severity of the sentences is not wholly congruent with the rank order based upon the maximum penalty allowed by statute. The normative scale underlying the former consists of several interconnected variables, each an aspect of the offender-victim relationship implicit in the definition of the offence, outlined as follows:

(1) The degree of specificity of the victim.

(2) The degree of direct contact between the offender and the victim.

(3) The extent to which the criminal act involves the element of bodily injury.

(a) Whether or not the element of bodily injury is an ingredient of the offender's intent.

(b) Whether the intent to do bodily injury is manifested merely in a threat, i.e., it is instrumental to some other criminal objective (as intimidating the victim in robbery), or is embodied in the infliction of physical injury.

(c) Whether the injury produces the victim's death.

The scale thus derived is termed *the degree of violation of the person*. Each successive element in the scale includes the preceding ones. The more elements involved in an offence, the higher its rank in terms of this scale, and the heavier its average penalty.

The next criterion in influence is the number of separate criminal acts, as measured by the number of bills of indictment, of which the defendant is convicted. This variable is significantly related to variation in the severity of sentences within each offence category.

The elements making up the prior criminal record in the order of their influence upon sentence variations are: the number of prior felony convictions, the number of misdemeanours disposed of by penitentiary sentences, and the number of misdemeanours disposed of by short terms of imprisonment or non-prison sentences. Each successive criterion is significant only in cases where it is the highest relevant criterion.

The recency of the last prior felony conviction bears a moderate though not statistically significant relationship to the variation in sentences, the more recent the conviction, the higher the sentence. This may reflect in part a judicial pique toward the offender who persists in his miscreancy. It also reflects the fact that defendants who have been lately convicted are more likely to be parole violators than those whose last conviction dates further back; hence they suffer an aggravation of the penalty.

The number of arrests not resulting in conviction has no effect whatever on the severity of the sentence.

A separate analysis of the criteria of the length of penitentiary sentences yields results which differ somewhat from those described above. The offence continues to be the most important determinant of the gravity of the sentence. The number of bills of indictment is also a significant factor except within the least serious offence category (misdemeanours) and the most serious offence category (felonious crimes against the person). The enormity of the prior criminal record, however, bears no significant relationship to the length of penitentiary sentences.

The hypothesis that legally irrelevant factors influence sentencing is tested by investigating the effects of sex, age, and race upon the severity of the penalties. The results demonstrate that the apparent preference accorded to females as compared with males, to youthful offenders as compared with mature offenders, and to whites as compared with Negroes is a function of differences in the patterns of criminal behaviour linked with sex, age and race. The women are convicted, generally, of less serious crimes than the men. The younger offenders compared with the older offenders do not have as serious records of recidivism but tend, on the whole, to commit more serious crimes. The Negro defendants, on the average, are older than the whites, hence they have had more opportunity to acquire prior records. The two races also differ in the percentage distribution of crimes at different age-levels. They are least alike in the youngest age-group, the Negroes committing more crimes of violence. As the offenders of both races grow older, they become more alike with respect to the percentage distribution of offences. When these differences in criminal behaviour patterns are held constant, the differences in sentences between male and female, young and old, or white and Negro become negligible.

The degree of disparity in sentencing is investigated by comparing the sentences of the different judges in cases of approximately equal gravity. The disparity is most pronounced in the cases at an intermediate level of gravity, tapering off gradually as the cases approach the polarities of mildness or seriousness. In fact there is a surprisingly high degree of consistency among the judges in the length of the penitentiary sentences they impose. In cases of lesser gravity, there are no significant differences among the 21 judges; in the more serious cases, only one of the judges is appreciably out of line with the others.

Differences among prosecutors have no significant effect upon the severity of the sentences which a judge imposes.

Contrary to common belief, judges do not favour defendants who plead guilty over those who plead not guilty. Other things being equal, the differences in sentences between the two kinds of plea are very slight. An exception to the previous statement is afforded by cases of minor crimes against personal property wherein those who plead guilty receive generally milder sentences. In the author's opinion this lenience rewards the offer to make restitution, which more commonly accompanies a guilty plea, rather than the co-operation with the court represented by a plea of guilt.

An examination of the offence charged in relation to the nature of the criminal act committed by the offender yields no indication that the 'bargain' process of justice (the district attorney settles for a conviction of a lesser offence than that for which the offender is indictable in exchange for a guilty plea) is a common practice.

The content of the judge's remarks in imposing sentence — threats, admonitions, expressions of indignation, reasons given for the aggravation or mitigation of the penalty — are not necessarily reflective of the factors which in reality determine the sentence. It is more likely that such comment is for the purpose of impressing the defendant or bidding for public approval (these judges are elected officials).

The findings of the statistical analysis summarized above yield a picture of certain orderly processes underlying the application of the criteria for sentencing. These too appear reasonable in relation to the goals of criminal justice but not simply as direct responses to rules of substantive or procedural law or judicial custom. Instead they are psycho-social facts concerning the structure and process of the normative orientation, or frame of reference, in relation to which the judges assess the relative gravity of cases.

We are confronted here with the problem of normative discrimination in a setting wherein the formal standard of judgement, the statutory scale of offences, is indefinite, wanting both precision and logical coherence. The crucial question posed by this problem is whether the ambiguity and haziness in the formal standard carry over into the sentencing by the court. Our results have shown that the normative inconsistency in the penal code is not projected into the court's judgement of the relative gravity of the offences. The degree of sanction attached to the various offences is not determined by the legally defined properties of each offence considered separately. Rather the statutory scale of crimes undergoes a re-evaluation in the minds of the judges, wherein the incongruities are ironed out and the judicial scale of crimes emerges logically consistent in terms of a unifying social value — the inviolability of the person.

Likewise the various criteria by which the defendant's recidivism may be measured — such as the number of prior convictions for felony or for misdemeanour — are not applied haphazardly. The importance of each in practice is relative to its commonly recognized seriousness. Moreover, each of these elements does not contribute to the weight of the penalty in some constant ratio to the other. Oddly, the highest criterion applicable to a case tends to blot out the impressive effect of the lesser criteria, indicating, perhaps, an effort toward simplicity and clarity in attempting to establish standards in the administration of justice.

The fact that the effect of the prior criminal record upon the severity of the sentences varies with the gravity of the offence suggests a tendency toward unity in the judge's impression of the criminal nature of the defendant. This impression is not merely a summation of traits revealed by the offence and the past criminal record, rather it is a product of the interaction between them. The offender as a perpetrator of certain crime(s) is perceived against the background of his past activities in crime. We have seen that up to a certain degree of seriousness of the crime, the gravity of the prior criminal record bears a strong relationship to the severity of the sentence. As the crime achieves a high degree of seriousness, however, it tends to overshadow the effect of the prior criminal record. In other words, once the judge perceives the offender as the perpetrator of a heinous crime, he no longer regards him as a likely subject for clemency or primarily rehabilitative treatment regardless of his past good record.

The results of the investigation of the effect of legally irrelevant factors do not mar or efface the unfolding picture of the legal integrity of the sentencing process. The bulk of the comment on the administration of justice with respect to minority groups assumes that judges are no different from other categories of persons in their proneness to be prejudiced; that, ordinarily, lacking the training in social science that would make them aware of the class and ethnic biases of their personal backgrounds, they project their prejudices into their decisions. The cumulative evidence of research studies of prejudice shows, however, that not all individuals or categories of persons tend equally to be prejudiced.[1] Prejudices against minority groups and broad generalizations abound but whether they influence decisions, and, if so, to what degree, depends upon individual attitudes stemming from such factors as cultural background, group pressure, personality disposition, and situational circumstances. How intense such attitudes must be in order to produce discrimination has not been demonstrated in general, let alone for judges, who are bound by the law, by their oath of office, and by the tradition of which they are a product, to isolate their biases from their professional judgements.

The results concerning the disparities among the judges in

---

[1] Gordon W. Allport, *The Nature of Prejudice* (Cambridge, Massachusetts: Addison-Wesley Publishing Company, Inc., 1954).

sentencing are not as clear in their implications. As we have seen, uniformity as well as inconsistency characterize the sentences of the various judges, the latter being most conspicuous in cases of intermediate gravity. Ruling out the likelihood that individual prejudice against certain categories of the population is a significant factor, two alternative, though not mutually exclusive, interpretations of the disparity remain: individual differences among the judges in (1) scales of penal values and (2) in their impressions of the seriousness of cases. With reference to the former, there is little doubt that differences in social background, personality, and penal philosophy make individual judges react differently to cases of equivalent gravity. But to what extent we cannot say, since we have not analysed the individual sentencing records with respect to these factors. The form which the disparity assumes suggests, however, that only in cases of intermediate gravity could differences in legal philosophy and other factors less susceptible to analysis be a prominent influence affecting variations in sentences.

The peculiar nature of the distribution of the disparity lends support to the second hypothesis, namely that differences among the judges in their impressions of offenders, perhaps as much as differing standards of judgement, underlie the inconsistency in sentencing. In cases that are patently mild or grave, the defendant can be clearly perceived with respect to the nature of criminality which is measured by the criteria for sentencing. Hence there is a relatively high degree of concord among the judges. Conversely, in cases of intermediate gravity, ambiguity is more apt to characterize the judge's perception of the defendant with a resulting increase in disparity. This interpretation argues strongly for the need of more precise standards for sentencing or more information on convicted defendants than the judges readily possess, particularly in cases that are clearly neither mild nor grave.

To sum up, the results provide assurance that the deliberations of the sentencing judge are not at the mercy of his passions or prejudices but comply with the mandate of the law. The criteria for sentencing recognized in the law, the nature of the crime and the offender's prior criminal record, are the decisive determinants of the severity of the sentence. The conclusions which show that the various criteria and the elements of which they are constituted are part of a larger organic whole suggest that justice is not merely what the law says it is, or what the judges in responding to their private predilections wish it to be. Rather it is a psycho-social reality reflected in the striving to accommodate sensibly the various factors which the judges regard as legitimate claims upon their deliberations.

APPENDIX OF TABLES

LIST OF TABLES

TABLE I.—LEGAL CLASSIFICATION OF OFFENCES AND NUMBER OF CASES OF EACH OFFENCE

	Maximum statutory prison sentence	No. of cases
Misdemeanours		
Against the public	1 mth.-3 yrs.	
Fornication		9
Indecent exposure		10
Obscene literature		1
Prostitution and assignation; solicitation for prostitution		15
Bigamy		1
Corrupting morals of minor		16
Loitering and prowling		4
Resisting arrest		7
False alarm		3
Riot		3
Carrying concealed deadly weapons ..		54
Failure to stop after motor vehicle accident		6
Operating motor vehicle licence revoked		2
Operating motor vehicle intoxicated ..		51
Liquor violations		78
Lotteries		19
Against property	2-3 yrs.	
Malicious mischief		13
Bad cheques		20
Attempted larceny		10
Attempted burglary		10
Operating motor vehicle without consent of owner		27
Possession of burglary tools		9.
Against the person	2-3 yrs.	
Assault and battery		39
Aggravated assault and battery.. ..		92
Involuntary manslaughter		3
Felonies		
Against public morals and decency ..	5-10 yrs.	
Solicitation to commit sodomy		5
Sodomy		6
Against personal property	5 yrs. (except forgery; 10 yrs.)	
Receiving stolen goods		18
Larceny		160
Larceny of auto		59
Fraud		21
Burglary of auto		34
Forgery		17
Against real property	20 yrs.	
Burglary		309
Against property accompanied by menace or force	10-20 yrs.	
Robbery (2 degrees)		135

TABLE I (*continued*)

	Maximum statutory prison sentence	No. of cases
Felonies (continued)		
Violations of Narcotic drug laws	5 yrs. (for 1st offence)	93
Against the person	5–7 yrs.	
Mayhem		2
Assault to ravish		9
Assault to kill		20
Against the person	10 yrs. to life	
Assault to rob		3
Voluntary manslaughter		8
Rape		13
Murder — 1st and 2nd degree		17
Miscellaneous		5

TABLE 2.—RELATION OF GRADE OF CRIME TO SEVERITY OF SENTENCE

Sentence	Grade of Crime					
	Misdemeanour (max. sent. 1–3 yrs.)		Felony (max. sent. 5–7 yrs.)		Felony (max. sent. 10 yrs. and up)	
	No.	%	No.	%	No.	%
Prison: 12 mths. and up ..	52	10·3	116	26·5	186	37·5
Prison: 3–11½ mths. ..	140	27·8	153	34·9	175	35·3
Non-imprisonment ..	311	61·9	169	38·6	135	27·2
Total	503	100·0	438	100·0	496	100·0

$\chi^2 = 153·4$; P < 0·001; C = 0·31

TABLE 3.—DISTRIBUTION OF TYPES OF SENTENCES IN EACH OFFENCE CATEGORY

Class of Offence (maximum prison sentence under statute)	Sentence													
	Prison: 12 mths. and up		Prison: 3–11½ mths.		Prison: to 3 mths.		Probation		Fine		Suspended		Total	
	No.	%	No.	%	No.	%	No.	%	No.	%	No.	%	No.	%
Misdemeanour														
Public (3 yrs.) ..	18	6·4	62	22·1	88	31·4	33	11·8	59	21·1	20	7·2	280	100·0
Property (3 yrs.) ..	14	15·7	17	19·1	27	30·3	29	32·6	0	0·0	2	2·3	89	100·0
Person (3 yrs.) ..	20	14·9	61	45·5	30	22·4	19	14·2	0	0·0	4	3·0	134	100·0
Felony														
Property (5–10 yrs.) ..	60	19·4	115	37·2	76	24·6	51	16·5	0	0·0	7	2·3	309	100·0
Burglary (20 yrs.) ..	90	29·1	122	39·5	57	18·4	38	12·3	0	0·0	2	0·7	309	100·0
Drugs (5 yrs.) ..	37	39·9	28	30·0	7	7·5	18	19·4	1	1·1	2	2·1	93	100·0
Robbery (10–20 yrs.) ..	61	45·2	45	33·3	12	8·9	14	10·4	0	0·0	3	2·2	135	100·0
*Person (5–7 yrs.) ..	19	61·3	10	25·8	5	9·7	2	3·2	0	0·0	0	0·0	36	100·0
†Person (10 yrs. and up) ..	32	68·1	8	17·0	2	4·3	5	10·6	0	0·0	0	0·0	47	100·0
Miscellaneous ..	3	60·0	0	0·0	1	20·0	0	0·0	0	0·0	1	20·0	5	100·0

* Includes 5 cases of solicitation to commit sodomy.   † Includes 6 cases of sodomy.

TABLE 4.—DISTRIBUTION OF SENTENCES FOR EACH FELONIOUS OFFENCE AGAINST THE PERSON

Offence (maximum prison sentence under statute)	Sentence							
	Prison: 12 mths. and up		Prison: 3–11½ mths.		Non-imprisonment		Total	
	No.	%	No.	%	No.	%	No.	%
Mayhem (5 yrs.)	0	0·0	2	100·0	0	0·0	2	100·0
Assault to ravish (5 yrs.)	6	66·7	3	33·3	0	0·0	9	100·0
Assault to kill (7 yrs.)	13	65·0	3	15·0	4	20·0	20	100·0
Assault to rob (10 yrs.) ..	1	33·3	1	33·3	1	33·3	3	100·0
Vol. Manslaughter (12 yrs.) ..	8	100·0	0	0·0	0	0·0	8	100·0
Rape (15 yrs.) ..	5	38·5	6	46·1	2	15·4	13	100·0
Murder: 1st and 2nd deg. (20 yrs. to life)	16	94·1	1	5·9	0	0·0	17	100·0

TABLE 5.—DISTRIBUTION OF SENTENCES FOR EACH FELONIOUS OFFENCE AGAINST PERSONAL PROPERTY

Offence	Sentence							
	Prison: 12 mths. and up		Prison: 3–11½ mths.		Non-imprisonment		Total	
	No.	%	No.	%	No.	%	No.	%
Larceny auto ..	7	11·9	24	40·7	28	47·4	59	100·0
Receiving stolen goods	3	16·7	9	50·0	6	33·3	18	100·0
Larceny	27	16·9	58	36·3	75	46·8	160	100·0
Forgery	3	17·6	6	35·3	8	47·1	17	100·0
Burglary auto ..	11	32·4	11	32·4	12	35·2	34	100·0
Fraud	8	38·1	7	33·3	6	28·6	21	100·0

$$\chi^2 = 13\cdot1; \ 0\cdot30 > P > 0\cdot20$$

TABLE 6.—DISTRIBUTION OF CASES OF EACH FELONIOUS OFFENCE AGAINST PERSONAL PROPERTY ACCORDING TO NUMBER OF PRIOR FELONY CONVICTIONS

| Offence | Number of prior convictions of felony | | | | | | | |
| | 0 | | 1 | | 2 and up | | Total | |
	No.	%	No.	%	No.	%	No.	%
Larceny auto ..	24	40·7	16	27·1	19	32·2	59	100·0
Receiving stolen goods	9	50·0	2	11·1	7	38·9	18	100·0
Larceny	65	40·6	39	24·4	56	35·0	160	100·0
Forgery	5	29·4	4	23·5	8	47·1	17	100·0
Burglary auto ..	15	44·1	7	20·6	12	35·3	34	100·0
Fraud	10	47·6	4	19·1	8	47·1	21	100·0

TABLE 7.—DISTRIBUTION OF CASES OF EACH FELONIOUS OFFENCE AGAINST PERSONAL PROPERTY ACCORDING TO NUMBER OF BILLS OF INDICTMENT ON WHICH DEFENDANT IS CONVICTED

| Offence | Number of indictments | | | | | | | |
| | 1 | | 2 | | 3 and up | | Total | |
	No.	%	No.	%	No.	%	No.	%
Larceny auto ..	9	15·3	39	66·1	11	18·6	59	100·0
Receiving stolen goods	12	66·7	5	27·8	1	5·5	18	100·0
Larceny	109	68·1	33	20·6	18	11·3	160	100·0
Forgery	2	11·8	5	29·4	10	58·8	17	100·0
Burglary auto ..	15	44·1	14	41·2	5	14·7	34	100·0
Fraud	7	33·3	4	19·1	10	47·6	21	100·0

TABLE 8.—RELATION OF NUMBER OF BILLS OF INDICTMENT ON WHICH DEFENDANT IS CONVICTED TO SEVERITY OF SENTENCE

| Sentence | Number of bills of indictment | | | | | | | |
| | 1 | | 2 | | 3 | | 4 and up | |
	No.	%	No.	%	No.	%	No.	%
Prison								
12 mths. and up	125	15·2	99	27·1	34	40·4	96	57·8
3–11½ mths. ..	269	32·7	144	39·5	26	31·0	29	17·5
to 3 mths. ..	221	26·9	60	16·4	11	13·1	13	7·8
Probation	129	15·7	47	12·9	11	13·1	22	13·3
Fine	48	5·8	9	2·5	1	1·2	2	1·2
Suspended— ..	30	3·7	6	1·6	1	1·2	4	2·4
Total ..	822	100·0	365	100·0	84	100·0	166	100·0

χ^2 (combining prison: to 3 mths. and sentences of non-imprisonment df = 6) = 170·9. P < 0·001; C = 0·32.

TABLE 9.—RELATION OF NUMBER OF PRIOR MISDEMEANOUR CONVICTIONS TO SEVERITY OF SENTENCE WITH NUMBER OF PRIOR FELONY CONVICTIONS CONTROLLED

Sentence	Number of prior misdemeanour convictions					
	0–1		2–3		4 and up	
	No.	%	No.	%	No.	%
A. 0 prior convictions of felony						
Prison: 12 mths. and up	69	13·1	15	16·0	16	21·6
Prison: 3–11½ mths.	130	24·8	31	33·0	30	40·6
Non-imprisonment	326	62·1	48	51·0	28	37·8
Total	525	100·0	94	100·0	74	100·0

$\chi^2 = 17\cdot8$; P<0·001

Sentence	0–1		2–3		4 and up	
	No.	%	No.	%	No.	%
B. 1 prior felony conviction						
Prison: 12 mths. and up ..	65	30·2	13	19·1	11	25·0
Prison: 3–11½ mths.	82	38·2	22	32·4	16	36·4
Non-imprisonment	68	31·6	33	48·5	17	38·6
Total	215	100·0	68	100·0	44	100·0

$\chi^2 = 7\cdot1$; 0·20>P>0·10

Sentence	0–1		2–3		4 and up	
	No.	%	No.	%	No.	%
C. 2 prior felony convictions						
Prison: 12 mths. and up ..	40	34·5	15	42·9	10	31·2
Prison: 3–11½ mths.	44	37·9	12	34·3	14	43·8
Non-imprisonment	32	27·6	8	22·8	8	25·0
Total	116	100·0	35	100·0	32	100·0

$\chi^2 = 1\cdot4$; 0·90>P>0·80

Sentence	0–1		2–3			
	No.	%	No.	%		
D. 3 prior felony convictions						
Prison: 12 mths. and up	21	36·2	8	23·5		
Prison: 3–11½ mths.	30	51·7	18	53·0		
Non-imprisonment	7	12·1	8	23·5		
Total	58	100·0	34	100·0		

$\chi^2 = 2\cdot9$; 0·30>P>0·20

Sentence	0–1		2–3			
	No.	%	No.	%		
E. More than 3 prior felony convictions						
Prison: 12 mths. and up	64	52·0	8	40·0		
Prison: 3–11½ mths.	32	26·0	7	35·0		
Non-imprisonment	27	22·0	5	25·0		
Total	123	100·0	20	100·0		

$\chi^2 = 1\cdot1$; 0·70>P>0·50

TABLE 10.—RELATION OF NUMBER OF PRIOR FELONY CONVICTIONS TO SEVERITY OF SENTENCE

Sentence	Number of prior convictions of felony									
	0		1		2		3		4 and up	
	No.	%	No.	%	No.	%	No.	%	No.	%
Prison 12 and up ..	100	14·4	88	27·0	65	35·5	28	31·5	73	50·7
3–11½ ..	191	27·7	120	36·8	70	38·3	48	52·2	39	27·1
to 3	196	28·2	60	18·4	24	13·1	7	7·6	18	12·5
Probation ..	151	21·8	32	9·8	16	8·7	4	4·3	6	4·2
Fine	36	5·2	15	4·6	3	1·6	3	3·3	8	2·1
Suspended ..	19	2·7	11	3·4	5	2·8	1	1·1	5	3·4·
Total ..	693	100·0	326	100·0	183	100·0	91	100·0	144	100·0

χ^2 (combining prison to 3 mths. and sentences of non-imprisonment) = 196·1; P < 0·001; C = 0·35

TABLE 11.—RELATION OF NUMBER OF PRIOR PENITENTIARY SENTENCES TO SEVERITY OF SENTENCE WITH NUMBER OF PRIOR FELONY CONVICTIONS CONTROLLED

Sentence	Number of prior penitentiary sentences							
	0		1–2					
	No.	%	No.	%				
A. 0 prior felony convictions								
Prison: 12 mths. and up	83	13·1	17	29·8				
Prison: 3–11½ mths. ..	170	26·7	21	36·8				
Non-imprisonment ..	383	60·2	19	33·4				
Total	636	100·0	57	100·0				
$\chi^2 = 18\cdot8$; P<0·001								

Sentence	0		1		2 and up			
B. 1 prior felony conviction								
Prison: 12 mths. and up	41	24·3	35	28·7	12	34·3		
Prison: 3–11½ mths. ..	66	39·0	43	35·2	11	31·4		
Non-imprisonment ..	62	36·7	44	36·1	12	34·3		
Total	169	100·0	122	100·0	35	100·0		
$\chi^2 = 1\cdot9$; 0·80>P>0·70								

Sentence	0		1		2 and up			
C. 2 prior felony convictions								
Prison: 12 mths. and up	22	31·9	26	36·6	17	39·5		
Prison: 3–11½ mths. ..	31	44·9	28	39·4	11	25·6		
Non-imprisonment ..	16	23·2	17	24·0	15	34·9		
Total	69	100·0	71	100·0	43	100·0		
$\chi^2 = 4\cdot6$; 0·50>P>0·30								

Sentence	0		1		2 and up			
D. 3 prior felony convictions								
Prison: 12 mths. and up	8	25·8	9	36·0	12	33·3		
Prison: 3–11½ mths. ..	20	64·5	14	56·0	14	38·9		
Non-imprisonment ..	3	9·7	2	8·0	10	27·8		
Total	31	100·0	25	100·0	36	100·0		
$\chi^2 = 7\cdot4$; 0·20>P>0·10								

Sentence	0–1		2		3		4 and up	
E. More than 3 prior felony convictions								
Prison: 12 mths. and up	24	58·5	17	42·5	10	43·5	21	53·8
Prison: 3–11½ mths. ..	11	26·8	12	30·0	7	30·4	9	23·1
Non-imprisonment ..	6	14·6	11	27·5	6	26·1	9	23·1
Total	41	100·0	40	100·0	23	100·0	39	100·0
$\chi^2 = 3\cdot6$; 0·80>P>0·70								

TABLE 12.—RELATION OF NUMBER OF PRIOR MISDEMEANOUR CONVICTIONS TO SEVERITY OF SENTENCE IN CASES WITH NO PRIOR FELONY CONVICTION WITH NUMBER OF PRIOR CONVICTIONS RESULTING IN PENITENTIARY SENTENCES CONTROLLED

Sentence	Number of prior misdemeanour convictions			
	0–2		3 and up	
	No.	%	No.	%
A. *No prior convictions resulting in penitentiary sentence*				
Prison: 12 mths. and up	66	11·9	17	20·5
Prison: 3–11½ mths. ..	142	25·7	28	33·7
Non-imprisonment ..	345	62·4	38	45·8
Total	553	100·0	83	100·0
$\chi^2 = 9\cdot1$; $0\cdot02 > P > 0.01$				
B. *1–2 prior convictions resulting in penitentiary sentence*				
Prison: 12 mths. and up	8	26·7	9	33·3
Prison: 3–11½ mths. ..	10	33·3	11	40·7
Non-imprisonment ..	12	40·0	7	26·7
Total	30	100·0	27	100·0
$\chi^2 = 1\cdot2$; $0\cdot70 > P > 0\cdot50$				

TABLE 13.—RELATION OF NUMBER OF ARRESTS NOT RESULTING IN CONVICTION TO SEVERITY OF SENTENCE WITH NUMBER OF PRIOR CONVICTIONS CONTROLLED

Sentence	Number of prior arrests					
	0		1–2		3 and up	
	No.	%	No.	%	No.	%
A. *0 prior convictions*						
Prison: 12 mths. and up	31	14·2	12	9·9	4	12·1
Prison: 3–11½ mths. ..	41	18·8	29	24·0	10	30·3
Non-imprisonment ..	146	67·0	80	66·1	19	57·6
Total	218	100·0	121	100·0	33	100·0
$\chi^2 = 3\cdot6$; $0\cdot50 > P > 0\cdot30$						

TABLE 13 (continued)

	Number of prior arrests					
	0·1		2 and up			
B. *1 prior conviction*						
Prison: 12 mths. and up	42	22·5	21	22·8		
Prison: 3–11½ mths.	62	33·2	32	34·8		
Non-imprisonment ..	83	44·4	39	42·4		
Total	187	100·0	92	100·0		

$\chi^2 = 0.5$; $0.80 > P > 0.70$

	0		1–3		4 and up	
C. *2 prior convictions*						
Prison: 12 mths. and up	11	20·8	34	27·2	11	35·5
Prison: 3–11½ mths. ..	20	37·7	51	40·8	11	35·5
Non-imprisonment ..	22	41·5	40	32·0	9	29·0
Total	53	100·0	125	100·0	31	100·0

$\chi^2 = 3.2$; $0.70 > P > 0.50$

	0–2		3 and up			
D. *3 prior convictions*						
Prison: 12 mths. and up	33	28·9	13	24·5		
Prison: 3–11½ mths.	44	38·6	23	43·4		
Non-imprisonment ..	37	32·5	17	32·1		
Total	114	100·0	53	100·0		

$\chi^2 = 0.5$; $0.80 > P > 0.70$

	0–1		2 and up			
E. *4 prior convictions*						
Prison: 12 mths. and up	22	34·9	12	32·4		
Prison: 3–11½ mths. ..	20	31·7	12	32·4		
Non-imprisonment ..	21	33·4	13	35·2		
Total	63	100·0	37	100·0		

$\chi^2 = 0.0$; $P = 1.0$

	0–1		2 and up			
F. *5 prior convictions*						
Prison: 12 mths. and up	14	37·8	24	37·5		
Prison: 3–11½ mths. ..	12	32·4	25	39·1		
Non-imprisonment ..	11	29·8	15	23·4		
Total:	37	100·0	64	100·0		

$\chi^2 = 0.6$; $0.80 > P > 0.70$

	0–3		4 and up			
G. *6 prior convictions*						
Prison: 12 mths. and up	16	29·6	54	35·1		
Prison: 3–11½ mths. ..	21	38·9	57	37·0		
Non-imprisonment ..	17	31·5	43	27·9		
Total	54	100·0	154	100·0		

$\chi^2 = 0.4$; $0.90 > P > 0.80$

TABLE 14.—RELATION OF RECENCY OF LAST PRIOR FELONY CONVICTION TO SEVERITY OF SENTENCE WITH NUMBER OF PRIOR FELONY CONVICTIONS CONTROLLED

Sentence	Years elapsed since last felony conviction					
	0–2		3–4		5 and up	
	No.	%	No.	%	No.	%
A. 1 prior conviction of felony						
Prison: 12 mths. and up	27	26·5	23	31·9	38	25·0
Prison: 3–11½ mths. ..	44	43·1	24	33·3	52	32·9
Non-imprisonment ..	31	30·4	25	34·8	62	42·1
Total	102	100·0	72	100·0	152	100·0
$\chi^2 = 4\cdot4$; $0\cdot50 > P > 0\cdot30$						
B. 2 prior convictions of felony						
Prison: 12 mths. and up	32	41·0	7	21·9	26	35·6
Prison: 3–11½ mths. ..	28	35·9	15	46·9	27	37·0
Non-imprisonment ..	18	23·1	10	31·2	20	27·4
Total	78	100·0	32	100·0	73	100·0
$\chi^2 = 3\cdot8$; $0\cdot50 > P > 0\cdot30$						
C. 3 prior convictions of felony						
Prison: 12 mths. and up	11	26·2	8	38·1	9	32·1
Prison: 3–11½ mths. ..	27	64·3	9	42·9	12	42·9
Non-imprisonment ..	4	9·5	4	19·0	7	25·0
Total	42	100·0	21	100·0	28	100·0
$\chi^2 = 5\cdot0$; $0\cdot30 > P > 0\cdot20$						
D. More than 3 prior convictions of felony						
Prison: 12 mths. and up	31	60·8	16	42·1	26	47·3
Prison: 3–11½ mths. ..	15	29·4	12	31·6	12	21·8
Non-imprisonment ..	5	9·8	10	26·3	17	30·9
Total	51	100·0	38	100·0	55	100·0
$\chi^2 = 8\cdot4$; $0\cdot10 > P > 0\cdot05$						

TABLE 15.—DISTRIBUTION OF PENITENTIARY SENTENCES OF VARIOUS
LENGTH IN EACH OFFENCE CATEGORY

Offence and max. sent. according to statute	Number of years									
	5 and up		3–5		2–3		1–2		Total	
	No.	%	No.	%	No.	%	No.	%	No.	%
Misdemeanour Public (to 3 yrs.) ..	0	0·0	0	0·0	0	0·0	19	100·0	19	100·0
Property (to 3 yrs.) ..	0	0·0	0	0·0	3	23·1	11	76·9	14	100·0
Person (to 3 yrs.) ..	0	0·0	2	10·0	1	5·0	17	85·0	20	100·0
Felony Property (5–10 yrs.) ..	2	3·3	4	6·7	10	16·7	44	73·3	60	100·0
Burglary (20 yrs.)	13	14·5	10	11·1	21	23·3	46	51·1	90	100·0
Drugs. (5 yrs.)	6	16·2	6	16·2	6	16·2	19	51·4	37	100·0
Robbery (10–20 yrs.) ..	16	26·3	11	18·0	12	19·7	22	36·0	61	100·0
Person (5–7 yrs.) ..	0	0·0	2	10·5	5	26·3	12	63·2	19	100·0
Person (10 yrs.–life) ..	14	43·8	4	12·5	3	9·4	11	34·4	32	100·0
Miscellaneous ..	0	0·0	0	0·0	1	50·0	1	50·0	2	100·0

TABLE 16.—RELATION OF NUMBER OF PRIOR FELONY CONVICTIONS TO LENGTH OF PENITENTIARY SENTENCE

Minimum sentence (in months)	Prior felony convictions					
	0–1		2–3		4 and up	
	No.	%	No.	%	No.	%
60 and up	27	14·4	14	15·0	20	13·7
36–59	18	9·6	8	8·6	13	17·8
24–35	33	17·5	13	14·0	10	21·9
12–23	110	58·5	58	62·4	34	46·6
Total	188	100·0	93	100·0	73	100·0

$$\chi^2 = 5\cdot9; \ 0\cdot50 > P > 0\cdot30$$

TABLE 17.—RELATION OF NUMBER OF BILLS OF INDICTMENT ON WHICH DEFENDANT IS CONVICTED TO LENGTH OF PENITENTIARY SENTENCE

Minimum sentence (in months)	Bills of Indictment					
	1–2		3–4		5 and up	
	No.	%	No.	%	No.	%
60 and up	23	10·3	8	14·6	20	26·7
36–59	20	8·9	7	12·7	11	16·0
24–35	33	14·7	17	30·9	13	16·0
12–23	148	66·1	23	41·8	31	41·3
Total	224	100·0	55	100·0	75	100·0

$$\chi^2 = 28\cdot6; \ P < 0\cdot001$$

TABLE 18.—RELATION OF SEX DIFFERENCES TO SEVERITY OF SENTENCE

Sentence	Sex			
	Male		Female	
	No.	%	No.	%
Prison: 12 mths. and up	315	23·4	6	6·5
Prison: indeterminate ..	20	1·5	13	14·1
Prison: 3–11½ mths. ..	448	33·3	20	21·7
Prison: to 3 mths. ..	288	21·3	17	19·6
Probation	187	13·9	22	23·9
Fine	53	3·9	7	7·6
Suspended	35	2·7	6	6·6
Total	1346	100·0	91	100·0

χ^2 (combining prison; 12 mths. and up with prison: indeterminate and prison to 3 mths. with sentences of non-imprisonment; $df = 2$) $= 9\cdot1$; $0\cdot02 > P > 0\cdot01$

TABLE 19.—DISTRIBUTION OF CASES BY SEX AND TYPE OF OFFENCE

Offence	Sex			
	Male		Female	
	No.	%	No.	%
Felonies				
Person	75	5·6	8	8·7
Robbery	128	9·5	7	7·6
Burglary	307	22·8	2	3·3
Drug Violations ..	79	5·9	14	15·2
Personal Property ..	290	21·6	19	19·6
Misdemeanours ..	462	34·3	41	45·6
Miscellaneous	5	0·3	0	0·0
Total	1346	100·0	91	100·0

$$\chi^2 = 34 \cdot 5; \ P < 0 \cdot 001$$

TABLE 20.—RELATION OF SEX TO SEVERITY OF SENTENCE IN CASES WITH NO PRIOR FELONY CONVICTION WITH GRADE OF CRIME CONTROLLED

Sentence	Sex			
	Male		Female	
	No.	%	No.	%
A. Felonies				
Prison: 12 mths. and up	74	20·1	6	20·7
Prison: 3–11½ mths. ..	117	31·7	8	27·6
Non-imprisonment ..	178	48·2	15	51·7
Total	369	100·0	29	100·0

$$\chi^2 = 0 \cdot 02; \ P = 0 \cdot 99$$

Sentence	Male No.	Male %	Female No.	Female %
B. Misdemeanours				
Prison: 12 mths. and up	18	7·0	2	5·3
Prison: 3–11½ mths. ..	60	23·3	6	15·8
Non-imprisonment ..	179	69·7	30	78·9
Total	257	100·0	38	100·0

$$\chi^2 = 1 \cdot 45; \ 0 \cdot 50 > P > 30$$

TABLE 21.—RELATION OF AGE DIFFERENCES TO SEVERITY OF SENTENCE

Sentence	Age					
	Under 21		21–29		30 and up	
	No.	%	No.	%	No.	%
Prison: 12 mths. and up..	47	22·9	154	24·4	151	25·5
Prison: 3–11½ mths. ..	54	26·3	232	36·8	180	30·4
Prison: to 3 mths. ..	41	20·0	114	18·1	149	25·1
Probation	51	24·9	98	15·5	59	9·9
Fine	2	1·0	19	3·0	38	6·4
Suspended	10	4·9	14	2·2	16	2·7
Total	205	100·0	631	100·0	593	100·0

$$\chi^2 = 60\cdot3; \text{ P} < 0\cdot001$$

TABLE 22.—RELATION OF AGE TO NUMBER OF PRIOR FELONY CONVICTIONS

Number of prior felony convictions	Age					
	Under 21		21–29		30 and up	
	No.	%	No.	%	No.	%
4 and up	1	0·5	36	5·7	106	17·9
3	7	3·4	42	6·7	42	7·1
2	16	7·8	83	13·3	83	14·0
1	44	21·5	162	25·6	119	20·1
0	137	66·8	308	48·7	243	40·9
Total	205	100·0	631	100·0	593	100·0

$$\chi^2 = 106\cdot6; \text{ P} < 0\cdot001$$

TABLE 23.—DISTRIBUTION OF CASES BY AGE AND TYPE OF OFFENCE

Offence	Age					
	Under 21		21–29		30 and up	
	No.	%	No.	%	No.	%
Person	12	5·8	24	3·8	48	8·1
Robbery	39	19·0	71	11·3	24	4·0
Burglary	47	22·9	157	25·0	105	17·7
Drugs	4	2·0	54	8·6	35	5·9
Property	50	24·4	132	21·0	127	21·4
Misdemeanours	53	25·9	191	30·3	254	42·9
Total	205	100·0	629	100·0	593	100·0

$$\chi^2 = 88\cdot7; \text{ P} < 0\cdot001$$

TABLE 24.—RELATION OF AGE TO SEVERITY OF SENTENCE IN BURGLARY CASES WITH NO PRIOR FELONY CONVICTION

Sentence	Age					
	Under 21		21–29		30 and up	
	No.	%	No.	%	No.	%
Prison: 12 mths. and up ..	5	17·8	7	11·3	2	6·7
Prison: 3–11½ mths. ..	7	25·0	21	33·9	8	26·7
Prison: to 3 mths.	8	28·6	17	27·4	13	43·3
Probation	8	28·6	17	27·4	7	23·3
Total	28	100·0	62	100·0	30	100·0

$$\chi^2 = 4·0; \ 0·30 > P > 0·20$$

TABLE 25.—RELATION OF AGE TO SEVERITY OF SENTENCE IN ROBBERY CASES WITH NO PRIOR FELONY CONVICTION

Sentence	Age			
	Under 21		21 and up	
	No.	%	No.	%
Prison: 12 mths. and up ..	9	34·6	15	31·3
Prison: 3–11½ mths. ..	7	26·7	22	45·8
Non-imprisonment ..	10	38·7	11	22·9
Total	26	100·0	48	100·0

$$\chi^2 = 2·9; \ 0·30 > P > 0·20$$

TABLE 26.—RELATIONSHIP OF AGE TO SEVERITY OF SENTENCE IN CASES OF AGGRAVATED ASSAULT AND BATTERY WITH NO PRIOR FELONY CONVICTION

Sentence	Age			
	Under 30		30 and up	
	No.	%	No.	%
Prison: 12 mths. and up ..	4	13·8	5	21·8
Prison: 3–11½ mths. ..	12	41·4	9	39·1
Non-imprisonment ..	13	44·8	9	39·1
Total	29	100·0	23	100·0

$$\chi^2 = 0·6; \ 0·80 > P > 0·70$$

TABLE 27.—RELATION OF RACE DIFFERENCE TO SEVERITY OF
SENTENCE

Sentence	Race			
	White		Negro	
	No.	%	No.	%
Prison: 12 mths. and up ..	87	26·1	266	24·3
Prison: 3–11½ mths. ..	93	27·9	370	33·9
Prison: to 3 mths. ..	71	21·3	232	21·3
Probation	67	20·1	140	12·8
Fine	5	1·5	53	4·9
Suspended	10	3·1	31	2·8
Total	333	100·0	1,092	100·0

$\chi^2 = 20·5$; $P < 0·01$
χ^2 (combining Prison to 3 months and sentences of non-
imprisonment, df = 2) = 4·2; $0·20 > P > 0·10$

TABLE 28.—DISTRIBUTION OF CASES BY RACE AND AGE

Age	Race			
	White		Negro	
	No.	%	No.	%
Under 21	67	20·2	137	12·6
21–29	134	40·5	492	45·1
30 and up	130	39·3	461	42·3
Total	331	100·0	1,090	100·0

$\chi^2 = 11·8$; $P < 0·01$

TABLE 29.—DISTRIBUTION OF CASES, AGE CONTROLLED, BY RACE
AND TYPE OF OFFENCE

Offence	Race			
	White		Negro	
	No.	%	No.	%
A. Under 21				
Person	2	3·0	10	7·3
Robbery	6	8·9	33	24·1
Burglary	24	35·8	22	16·1
Drugs	2	3·0	2	1·5
Theft	14	20·9	36	26·2
Misdemeanour ..	19	28·4	34	24·8
Total	67	100·0	137	100·0
B. 21–29				
Person	5	3·7	19	3·8
Robbery	15	11·1	56	11·5
Burglary	40	29·9	116	23·7
Drugs	3	2·2	51	10·2
Theft	37	27·6	94	19·3
Misdemeanour ..	34	25·5	154	31·5
Total	134	100·0	490	100·0
C. 30 and up				
Person	10	7·8	38	8·2
Robbery	5	3·9	19	4·1
Burglary	24	18·6	80	17·4
Drugs	4	3·1	30	6·5
Theft	39	30·2	88	19·1
Misdemeanour ..	47	36·4	206	44·7
Total	129	100·0	461	100·0

TABLE 30.—RELATION OF RACE DIFFERENCE TO SEVERITY OF SENTENCE IN CASES OF BURGLARY WITH NUMBER OF PRIOR FELONY CONVICTIONS CONTROLLED

Sentence	Race			
	White		Negro	
	No.	%	No.	%
A. 0 prior convictions of felony				
Prison: 12 mths. and up	4	10·8	11	13·3
Prison: 3–11½ mths. ..	11	29·7	25	30·1
Prison: to 3 mths. ..	10	27·0	27	32·5
Probation	12	32·5	20	24·1
Total	37	100·0	83	100·0

$$\chi^2 = 1·0; \ 0·90 > P > 0·80$$

Sentence	White		Negro	
B. 1 or more prior convictions of felony				
Prison: 12 mths. and up	24	45·3	51	38·1
Prison: 3—11½ mths. ..	17	32·1	68	50·1
Prison: to 3 mths. ..	8	15·1	11	8·2
Probation and Suspended	4	7·5	4	2·9
Total	53	100·0	134	100·0

$$\chi^2 = 4·9; \ 0·20 > P > 0·10$$

TABLE 31.—RELATION OF RACE DIFFERENCES TO SEVERITY OF SENTENCE IN CASES OF ROBBERY WITH 0–1 PRIOR FELONY CONVICTION

Sentence	Race			
	White		Negro	
	No.	%	No.	%
Prison: 12 mths. and up ..	13	48·2	48	44·9
Prison: 3–11½ mths. ..	7	25·9	38	35·5
Non-imprisonment ..	7	25·9	21	19·6
Total	27	100·0	107	100·0

$$\chi^2 = 1·1; \ 0·70 > P > 0·50$$

TABLE 32.—RELATION OF RACE DIFFERENCES TO SEVERITY OF SENTENCE IN FELONIOUS CRIMES AGAINST PERSONAL PROPERTY WITH NUMBER OF PRIOR FELONY CONVICTIONS CONTROLLED

Sentence	Race			
	White		Negro	
	No.	%	No.	%
(1) *0–1 prior convictions of felony*				
Prison: 12 mths. and up	8	13·8	12	8·6
Prison: 3–11½ mths. ..	16	27·6	52	37·4
Prison: to 3 mths.. ..	21	36·2	41	30·2
Probation and Suspended	13	22·4	33	23·8
Total	58	100·0	138	100·0

$$\chi^2 = 2\cdot8; \ 0\cdot50 > P > 0\cdot30$$

Sentence	Race			
(2) *2 or more prior convictions of felony*				
Prison: 12 mths. and up	13	40·6	27	34·2
Prison: 3–11½ mths. ..	9	28·1	38	48·1
Prison: to 3 mths. ..	4	12·5	9	11·4
Probation and Suspended	6	18·7	5	6·3
Total	32	100·0	79	100·0

$$\chi^2 = 5\cdot9; \ 0\cdot20 > P > 0\cdot10$$

TABLE 33.—RELATION OF RACE DIFFERENCES TO SEVERITY OF SENTENCE IN CASES OF MISDEMEANOURS (LIQUOR AND GAMBLING VIOLATIONS OMITTED)

Sentence	Race			
	White		Negro	
	No.	%	No.	%
Prison: 12 mths. and up ..	15	15·6	34	11·2
Prison: 3–11½ mths. ..	27	28·1	92	30·4
Prison: to 3 mths.	24	25·0	105	34·7
Probation	24	25·0	49	16·1
Fines and Suspended ..	6	6·3	23	7·6
Total	96	100·0	303	100·0

$$\chi^2 = 5\cdot5; \ 0\cdot30 > P > 0\cdot20$$

TABLE 34.—RELATION OF RACE DIFFERENCE TO SEVERITY OF SENTENCE IN CASES OF FELONIOUS CRIMES AGAINST PERSONAL PROPERTY AND MISDEMEANOURS WITH NO PRIOR CONVICTIONS

Sentence	Race			
	White		Negro	
	No.	%	No.	%
Prison: 12 mths. and up ..	5	11·6	6	3·6
Prison: 3–11½ mths. ..	9	21·0	28	17·0
Prison: to 3 mths... ..	12	27·9	59	35·8
Probation	12	27·9	50	30·3
Fines and Suspended ..	5	11·6	21	13·3
Total	43	100·0	164	100·0

$$^2\chi = 5\cdot0; \ 0\cdot30 > P > 0\cdot20$$

TABLE 35.—RELATION OF RACE DIFFERENCES TO LENGTH OF PENITENTIARY SENTENCE

Sentence (in months)	Race			
	White		Negro	
	No.	%	No.	%
60 and up	10	11·8	41	15·3
36–59	12	14·1	27	10·1
24–35	14	16·5	48	17·9
12–23	49	57·6	152	56·7
Total	85	100·0	268	100·0

$$\chi^2 = 1\cdot5; \ 0\cdot70 > P > 0\cdot50$$

TABLE 36.—DISTRIBUTION OF CASES OF NEGRO OFFENDERS ACCORDING TO REGION OF BIRTH (NORTH OR SOUTH) AND SEVERITY OF SENTENCE

Sentence	Region			
	North		South	
	No.	%	No.	%
Prison: 12 mths. and up ..	37	21·3	23	17·8
Prison: 3–11½ mths. ..	58	33·3	49	38·0
Prison: to 3 mths... ..	44	25·3	25	19·4
Probation	27	15·5	23	17·8
Fines and Suspended ..	8	4·6	9	7·0
Total	174	100·0	129	100·0

$$\chi^2 = 3\cdot1; \ 0\cdot70 > P > 0\cdot50$$

I

TABLE 37.—PERCENTAGE OF EACH TYPE OF SENTENCE RECEIVED
BY WHITES, NORTHERN-BORN NEGROES AND SOUTHERN-BORN NEGROES

Sentence	Whites	Northern Negroes	Southern Negroes
Prison: 12 mths. and up	26·1	21·3	17·8
Prison: 3–11½ mths. ..	27·9	33·3	38·0
Non-imprisonment ..	46·0	45·4	44·2
Total	100·0	100·0	100·0

TABLE 38.—DISTRIBUTION OF CASES BY NUMBER OF PRIOR FELONY
CONVICTIONS AND NUMBER OF BILLS OF INDICTMENT

Number of prior convictions of felony	Number of bills of indictment							
	1		2		3		4 and up	
	No.	%	No.	%	No.	%	No.	%
0	417	50·7	166	45·4	40	47·6	70	42·2
1	172	20·9	90	24·7	22	26·2	42	25·3
2	101	12·3	47	12·9	9	10·7	26	15·7
3	53	6·4	24	6·6	3	3·6	11	6·6
4 and up	79	9·7	38	10·4	10	11·9	17	10·2
Total ..	822	100·0	365	100·0	84	100·0	166	100·0

$$\chi^2 = 11·1; \ 0·70 > P > 0·50$$

TABLE 39.—DISTRIBUTION OF CASES ACCORDING TO OFFENCE AND
NUMBER OF BILLS OF INDICTMENTS

Offence	Number of indictments									
	1		2		3		4			
	No.	%	No.	%	No.	%	No.	%	No.	%
Misdemeanours										
Public	220	78·6	47	16·8	8	2·9	5	1·7	280	100·0
Property	45	50·6	32	35·9	4	4·5	8	9·0	89	100·0
Person	106	79·1	23	17·2	3	2·2	2	1·5	134	100·0
Felonies										
Personal Property	153	49·5	86	27·8	15	4·9	55	17·8	309	100·0
Burglary	148	47·9	90	29·1	27	8·7	44	14·3	309	100·0
Drugs	61	65·6	24	25·8	3	3·2	5	5·4	93	100·0
Person (5–7 yrs.) ..	15	41·6	13	36·1	5	13·9	3	8·4	36	100·0
Robbery	43	31·8	39	28·9	16	11·9	37	27·4	135	100·0
Person (10 yrs–life)	26	55·3	12	25·5	3	6·4	6	12·8	47	100·0

TABLE 40.—DISTRIBUTION OF CASES ACCORDING TO OFFENCE AND NUMBER OF PRIOR FELONY CONVICTIONS

| Offence | Number of prior felony convictions | | | | | | | | | |
| | 0 | | 1 | | 2–3 | | 4 and up | | Total | |
	No.	%	No.	%	No.	%	No.	%	No.	%
Misdemeanours										
Public	174	62·1	56	20·0	36	12·9	14	5·0	280	100·0
Property	39	43·8	26	29·2	14	15·7	10	11·3	89	100·0
Person	82	61·2	27	20·1	20	14·9	5	3·8	134	100·0
Felonies										
Personal Property	127	41·1	71	23·0	64	20·7	47	15·2	309	100·0
Burglary	121	39·2	74	23·9	78	25·2	36	11·7	309	100·0
Drugs	30	32·3	18	19·4	27	29·0	18	19·3	93	100·0
Robbery	74	54·8	34	25·2	22	16·3	5	3·7	135	100·0
Person	44	53·0	19	22·9	13	15·7	7	8·4	83	100·0

TABLE 41.—DISTRIBUTION OF CASES BY SCORE AND SEVERITY OF SENTENCE

Score	Sentence							
	Non-imprisonment		3–11½ mths.		12 mths. and up		Total	
	No.	%	No.	%	No.	%	No.	%
58	—	0·0	—	0·0	2	100·0	2	100·0
53	3	9·7	2	6·5	26	83·8	31	100·0
52	—	0·0	—	0·0	3	100·0	3	100·0
51	—	0·0	—	0·0	7	100·0	7	100·0
50	—	0·0	—	0·0	10	100·0	10	100·0
49	2	10·5	3	15·8	14	73·7	19	100·0
48	9	13·6	15	22·7	42	63·7	66	100·0
47	1	10·0	1	10·0	8	80·0	10	100·0
46	4	15·8	8	42·1	8	42·1	19	100·0
45	4	11·1	11	30·6	21	58·3	36	100·0
44	18	25·4	22	31·0	31	43·6	71	100·0
43	3	12·0	11	44·0	11	44·0	25	100·0
42	4	8·0	21	42·0	25	50·0	50	100·0
41	11	22·0	26	52·0	13	26·0	50	100·0
40	25	23·4	57	53·2	25	23·4	107	100·0
39	17	25·8	32	48·4	17	25·8	66	100·0
38	11	22·4	17	34·7	21	42·9	49	100·0
37	32	37·2	39	45·3	15	17·4	86	100·0
36	10	30·3	18	54·5	5	15·2	33	100·0
35	45	53·6	31	36·9	8	9·5	84	100·0
34	61	54·5	37	33·0	14	12·5	112	100·0
33	67	63·2	31	29·2	8	7·6	106	100·0
32	9	69·2	2	15·4	2	15·4	13	100·0
31	40	64·5	19	30·6	3	4·9	62	100·0
30	10	43·5	8	34·8	5	21·7	23	100·0
29	12	80·0	3	20·0	—	0·0	15	100·0
28	86	72·9	27	22·9	5	4·2	118	100·0
26	112	78·3	26	18·2	5	3·5	143	100·0
23	20	95·2	1	4·8	—	0·0	21	100·0
Total	615		468		354		1437	

TABLE 42.—DISTRIBUTION OF CASES BY SCORE AND SEVERITY OF SENTENCE (CONTRACTED)

Score	Sentence							
	Prison: 12 mtns. and up		Prison: 3–11½ mths.		Non-imprisonment		Total	
	No.	%	No.	%	No.	%	No.	%
45	141	69·5	40	19·7	22	10·8	203	100·0
36–44	163	30·3	243	45·3	131	24·4	537	100·0
23–35	50	7·2	185	26·5	462	66·3	697	100·0
Total	354		468		615		1547	

$$\chi^2 = 486·7; \ P < 0·001; \ C = 0·503$$

TABLE 43.—DISTRIBUTION OF CASES BY JUDGE AND TYPE OF SENTENCE

Judge	Prison: 12 mths. and up		Prison: 3–11½ mths.		Prison: under 3 mths.		Probation		Fine		Suspended		Total	
	No.	%	No.	%	No.	%	No.	%	No.	%	No.	%	No.	%
A	8	14·1	22	38·6	17	29·8	6	10·5	0	0·0	4	7·0	57	100·0
B	10	40·0	3	12·0	9	36·0	0	0·0	3	12·0	0	0·0	25	100·0
C	14	17·3	32	39·5	12	14·8	19	23·5	4	4·9	0	0·0	81	100·0
D	1	3·8	12	46·2	6	23·1	2	7·7	4	15·4	1	3·8	26	100·0
E	8	14·0	32	56·1	5	8·8	5	8·8	4	7·0	3	5·3	57	100·0
F	7	13·0	21	38·9	15	27·8	8	14·8	3	5·5	0	0·0	54	100·0
G	72	25·5	68	24·0	70	24·7	59	20·8	4	1·4	10	3·6	283	100·0
H	19	38·0	17	34·0	0	0·0	8	16·0	3	6·0	3	6·0	50	100·0
I	33	41·3	30	37·5	13	16·3	2	2·5	1	1·2	1	1·2	80	100·0
J	27	34·6	30	38·5	6	7·7	6	7·7	5	6·4	4	5·1	78	100·0
K	9	19·1	28	59·6	3	6·4	3	6·4	4	8·5	0	0·0	47	100·0
L	12	23·1	24	46·2	7	13·5	6	11·5	1	1·9	2	3·8	52	100·0
M	30	44·8	17	25·3	13	19·4	5	7·5	1	1·5	1	1·5	67	100·0
N	15	34·9	8	18·6	18	41·9	0	0·0	2	4·6	0	0·0	43	100·0
O	46	25·0	42	22·8	39	21·2	44	23·9	8	4·4	5	2·7	184	100·0
P	20	10·4	66	34·4	69	35·9	24	12·5	8	4·2	5	2·6	192	100·0
Q	13	30·9	12	28·6	3	7·1	10	23·8	2	4·8	2	4·8	42	100·0
R	10	52·6	4	21·1	0	0·0	2	10·5	3	15·8	0	0·0	19	100·0

TABLE 44.—DISTRIBUTION OF CASES, SCORE 23–35, BY JUDGE AND TYPE OF SENTENCE

A. Judges ranking 1–13 in proportion of prison sentences imposed

Judge	Sentence							
	Prison: 12 mths. and up		Prison: 3–11½ mths.		Non-imprisonment		Total	
	No.	%	No.	%	No.	%	No.	%
C	0	0·0	6	17·6	28	82·4	34	100·0
F	0	0·0	5	21·4	23	78·6	28	100·0
P	4	3·8	20	19·2	80	77·0	104	100·0
B	2	16·7	1	8·3	9	75·0	12	100·0
A	0	0·0	6	26·1	17	73·9	23	100·0
G	8	6·3	26	20·3	94	73·4	128	100·0
O	7	6·3	23	20·7	81	73·0	111	100·0
Q	0	0·0	5	29·4	12	70·6	17	100·0
N	5	20·0	3	12·0	17	68·0	25	100·0
D	1	6·7	4	26·7	10	66·6	15	100·0
H	3	17·6	3	17·6	11	64·8	17	100·0
J	2	6·7	10	33·3	18	60·0	30	100·0
Total ..	32		112		400		544	
Rank of Type of Sentence	528·5		456·5		200·5			

H (corrected for ties) = 11·1 (df = 11); 0·50 > P > 0·30

B. Judges ranking 14–18 in proportion of prison sentences imposed

Judge	Prison: 12 mths. and up		Prison: 3–11½ mths.		Non-imprisonment		Total	
R	2	20·0	3	30·0	5	50·0	10	100·0
E	0	0·0	12	50·0	12	50·0	24	100·0
L	1	4·2	14	58·3	9	37·5	24	100·0
K	2	7·7	15	57·7	9	34·6	26	100·0
I	6	16·2	20	54·1	11	29·7	37	100·0
M	7	21·9	9	28·1	16	50·0	32	100·0
Total ..	18		73		62		153	
Rank of Type of Sentence	144·5		99·0		31·5			

H (corrected for ties) = 4·1 (df = 5); 0·30 > P > 0·20

TABLE 45.—DISTRIBUTION OF CASES, SCORE 36–44, BY JUDGE AND TYPE OF SENTENCE

A. Judges ranking 1–3 in proportion of prison sentences of a minimum of 12 months and up.

Judge	Sentence							
	Prison: 12 mths. and up		Prison: 3–11½ mths.		Non-imprisonment		Total	
	No.	%	No.	%	No.	%	No.	%
D	0	0·0	7	77·8	2	22·2	9	100·0
E	2	8·0	18	72·0	5	20·0	25	100·0
P	8	11·8	38	55·9	22	32·3	68	100·0
Total ..	10		63		29		102	
Rank of Type of Sentence	97·5		61·0		15·0			

H (corrected for ties) = 1·8 (df = 2); 0·50 > P > 0·30

B. Judges ranking 4–11 in proportion of prison sentences of a minimum of 12 months and up

Judge	Prison: 12 mths. and up		Prison: 3–11½ mths.		Non-imprisonment		Total	
C	7	18·4	24	63·2	7	18·4	38	100·0
F	4	20·0	16	80·0	0	0·0	20	100·0
A	6	21·4	7	50·0	4	28·6	14	100·0
Q	3	21·4	7	50·0	4	28·6	14	100·0
L	4	22·2	8	44·4	6	33·4	18	100·0
K	4	25·0	12	75·0	0	0·0	16	100·0
N	4	30·8	5	38·4	4	30·8	13	100·0
G	41	34·2	36	30·0	43	35·8	120	100·0
Total ..	73		122		72		267	
Rank of Type of Sentence	231·0		133·5		36·5			

H (corrected for ties) = 4·2 (df = 7); 0·80 > P > 0·70

C. Judges ranking 12–18 in proportion of prison sentences of a minimum of 12 months and up

Judge	Sentence							
	Prison: 12 mths. and up		Prison: 3–11½ mths.		Non-imprisonment		Total	
	No.	%	No.	%	No.	%	No.	%
H	7	38·9	8	44·4	3	16·7	18	100·0
M	8	42·1	7	36·8	4	21·1	19	100·0
O	23	41·2	17	32·7	12	23·1	52	100·0
J	13	44·8	14	48·3	2	6·9	29	100·0
B	5	50·0	2	20·0	3	30·0	10	100·0
I	20	57·1	9	25·7	6	17·1	35	100·0
R	4	80·0	1	20·0	0	0·0	5	100·0
Total ..	79		64		33		176	
Rank of Type of Sentence	137·0		65·5		17·0			

H (corrected for ties) = 9·2 (df = 6); 0·20 > P > 0·10

TABLE 46.—DISTRIBUTION OF CASES, SCORE 45–58, BY JUDGE AND TYPE OF SENTENCE

A. *Judges ranking 1–4 in proportion of prison sentences of a minimum of 12 months and up*

Judge	Sentence							
	Prison: 12 mths. and up		Prison: 3–11½ mths.		Non-imprisonment		Total	
	No.	%	No.	%	No.	%	No.	%
D	0	0·0	1	50·0	1	50·0	2	100·0
A	2	33·3	2	33·3	2	33·3	6	100·0
P	8	40·0	8	40·0	4	20·0	20	100·0
F	3	50·0	0	0·0	3	50·0	6	100·0
Total ..	13		11		10			
Rank of Type of Sentence ..	28·0		16·0		5·5			

H (Corrected for ties) = 1·5 (df = 3); 0·70 > P > 0·50

B. *Judges ranking 5–18 in proportion of prison sentences of a minimum of 12 months and up*

Judge	Prison: 12 mths. and up		Prison: 3–11½ mths.		Non-imprisonment		Total	
	No.	%	No.	%	No.	%	No.	%
K	3	60·0	1	20·0	1	20·0	5	100·0
J	12	63·2	6	31·6	1	5·2	19	100·0
G	23	65·8	6	17·1	6	17·1	35	100·0
H	9	64·3	5	35·7	0	0·0	14	100·0
L	7	70·0	2	20·0	1	10·0	10	100·0
E	6	75·0	2	25·0	0	0·0	8	100·0
O	16	76·2	3	14·3	2	9·5	21	100·0
C	7	77·8	2	22·2	0	0·0	9	100·0
I	7	87·5	1	12·5	0	0·0	8	100·0
Q	10	90·9	0	0·0	1	9·1	11	100·0
M	15	93·8	1	6·2	0	0·0	16	100·0
N	6	100·0	0	0·0	0	0·0	6	100·0
R	4	100·0	0	0·0	0	0·0	4	100·0
B	3	100·0	0	0·0	0	0·0	3	100·0
Total ..	128		29		12			
Rank of Type of Sentence ..	105·5		27·0		6·5			

H (Corrected for ties) = 14·3 (df = 13); 0·50 > P > 0·30

TABLE 47.—RELATION OF SCORE TO LENGTH OF PENITENTIARY SENTENCE

Score	Sentence							
	12–63		24–59		60 and up		Total	
	No.	%	No.	%	No.	%	No.	%
24–35	16	25·4	18	28·6	29	46·0	63	100·0
17–23	52	43·0	52	43·0	17	14·0	121	100·0
10–16	134	78·2	31	18·2	5	3·0	170	100·0
Total ..	202		101		51		354	

$$\chi^2 = 101·1; \; P < 0·001; \; C = 0·47$$

TABLE 48.—DISTRIBUTION OF CASES RECEIVING PENITENTIARY SENTENCES, SCORE 10–22, BY JUDGE AND LENGTH OF MINIMUM TERM

Judge	Sentence									
	12–23		24–35		36–59		60 and up		Total	
	No.	%	No.	%	No.	%	No.	%	No.	%
A	6	100·0	0	0·0	0	0·0	0	0·0	6	100·0
B	6	85·7	0	0·0	1	14·3	0	0·0	7	100·0
C	8	88·9	0	0·0	1	11·1	0	0·0	9	100·0
D	1	100·0	0	0·0	0	0·0	0	0·0	1	100·0
E	5	83·3	1	16·7	0	0·0	0	0·0	6	100·0
F	4	57·1	3	42·9	0	0·0	0	0·0	7	100·0
G	29	54·7	13	24·5	5	9·4	6	11·4	53	100·0
H	7	58·3	3	25·0	2	16·7	0	0·0	12	100·0
I	20	80·0	4	16·0	1	4·0	7	0·0	25	100·0
J	15	83·3	3	16·7	0	0·0	0	0·0	18	100·0
K	4	66·6	1	16·7	1	16·7	0	0·0	6	100·0
L	3	50·0	3	50·0	0	0·0	0	0·0	6	100·0
M	12	63·2	1	5·2	3	15·8	3	15·8	19	100·0
N	9	100·0	0	0·0	0	0·0	0	0·0	9	100·0
O	21	61·8	8	23·5	5	14·7	0	0·0	34	100·0
P	9	69·2	2	15·4	1	7·7	1	7·7	13	100·0
Q	3	75·0	1	25·0	0	0·0	0	0·0	4	100·0
R	4	80·0	1	20·0	0	0·0	0	0·0	5	100·0
Total ..	166		44		20		10		240	
Rank of Sentence	83·5		188·5		220·5		235·5			

H (corrected for ties) = 24·1 (df = 17); 0·20 > P > 0·10

TABLE 49.—DISTRIBUTION OF CASES RECEIVING PENITENTIARY SENTENCES, SCORE 23–35, BY JUDGE AND LENGTH OF MINIMUM TERM

Judge	Sentence									
	12–23		24–35		36–59		60 and up		Total	
	No.	%	No.	%	No.	%	No.	%	No.	%
A. All Judges except I										
M..	3	27·3	1	9·1	0	0·0	7	63·6	11	100·0
C..	2	40·0	0	0·0	0	0·0	3	60·0	5	100·0
Q..	2	22·2	0	0·0	3	33·3	4	44·5	9	100·0
N..	3	50·0	0	0·0	0	0·0	3	50·0	6	100·0
G..	5	26·3	2	10·5	3	15·8	9	47·4	19	100·0
O..	3	25·0	4	33·3	2	16·7	3	25·0	12	100·0
Others	6	40·0	3	20·0	1	6·7	5	33·3	15	100·0
L	3	50·0	2	33·3	0	0·0	1	16·7	6	100·0
J	3	33·3	1	11·1	4	44·5	1	11·1	9	100·0
P	2	28·6	4	57·1	1	14·3	0	0·0	7	100·0
H	4	57·1	2	28·6	1	14·3	0	0·0	7	100·0
Total	36		19		15		36		106	
Rank of Sentence	18·5		46·0		63·0		88·5			
H (corrected for ties) = 11·7 (df = 10); 0·50 > P > 0·30										
B. Judge I										
I	0	0·0	0	0·0	3	37·5	5	62·5	8	100·0

TABLE 50.—DISTRIBUTION OF CASES BY ASSISTANT DISTRICT ATTORNEY AND TYPE OF SENTENCE

Assistant District Attorney	Sentence							
	Prison: 12 mths. and up		Prison: 3–11½ mths.		Non-imprisonment		Total	
	No.	%	No.	%	No.	%	No.	%
a..	10	20·0	16	32·0	24	48·0	50	100·0
b..	6	35·3	5	29·4	6	35·3	17	100·0
c..	27	37·5	17	23·6	28	38·9	72	100·0
d..	9	42·9	4	19·0	8	38·1	21	100·0
e..	31	20·7	43	28·7	76	50·6	150	100·0
f	7	20·6	10	29·4	17	50·0	34	100·0
g..	9	18·0	15	30·0	26	52·0	50	100·0
h..	52	22·2	92	39·3	90	38·5	234	100·0
i	6	26·1	8	34·8	9	39·1	23	100·0
j	28	25·7	47	43·1	34	31·2	109	100·0
k..	18	23·7	20	26·3	38	50·0	76	100·0
l	83	21·0	148	37·5	164	41·5	395	100·0
m	37	29·6	30	24·0	58	46·4	125	100·0
n..	10	34·5	3	10·3	16	55·2	29	100·0
o (others)	21	40·4	10	19·2	21	40·4	52	100·0

$$\chi^2 = 61·5; \ P < 0·001$$

TABLE 51.—DISTRIBUTION OF CASES BY ASSISTANT DISTRICT ATTORNEY AND SEVERITY OF SENTENCE WITH JUDGE CONTROLLED

Assistant District Attorney	Prison: 12 mths. and up		Prison: 3–11½ mths.		Non-imprisonment		Total	
	No.	%	No.	%	No.	%	No.	%
A. *Judge G*								
c	15	31·9	9	19·1	23	49·0	47	100·0
e	11	24·4	10	22·2	24	53·4	45	100·0
h	7	15·6	11	24·4	27	60·0	45	100·0
l	13	29·5	12	27·3	19	43·2	44	100·0
m	25	29·1	16	18·6	45	52·3	86	100·0
$\chi^2 = 5\cdot3$; $0\cdot80 > P > 0\cdot70$								
B. *Judge I*								
j	15	37·5	15	37·5	10	25·0	40	100·0
l	15	51·7	10	34·5	4	13·8	29	100.0
$\chi^2 = 1\cdot7$; $0\cdot50 > P > 0\cdot30$								
C. *Judge J*								
h	13	30·2	19	44·2	11	25·6	43	100·0
i	6	26·1	8	34·7	9	39·2	23	100·0
$\chi^2 = 1\cdot3$; $0\cdot70 > P > 0\cdot50$								
D. *Judge L*								
e	6	26·1	8	34·8	9	39·1	23	100·0
j	5	17·8	16	57·2	7	25·0	28	100·0
$\chi^2 = 2\cdot6$; $0\cdot30 > P > 0\cdot20$								
E. *Judge M*								
c	11	45·8	9	37·5	4	16·7	24	100·0
k	8	34·8	5	21·8	10	43·4	23	100·0
$\chi^2 = 4\cdot2$; $0\cdot20 > P > 0\cdot10$								
F. *Judge O*								
a	6	20·0	5	16·7	19	63·3	30	100·0
k	10	21·3	10	21·3	27	57·4	47	100·0
l	13	25·0	18	34·6	21	40·4	52	100·0
$\chi^2 = 5\cdot4$; $0\cdot30 > P > 0\cdot20$								
G. *Judge P*								
a	4	20·0	9	45·0	7	35·0	20	100·0
e	7	13·2	17	32·1	29	54·7	53	100·0
$\chi^2 = 2\cdot2$; $0\cdot50 > P > 0\cdot30$								

TABLE 52.—DISTRIBUTION OF CASES ACCORDING TO PLEA AND
SEVERITY OF SENTENCE

Sentence	Plea			
	Guilty		Not Guilty	
	No.	%	No.	%
Prison: 12 mths. and up	197	29·9	157	20·2
Prison: 3–11½ mths. ..	189	28·6	279	35·9
Non-imprisonment ..	274	41·5	341	43·9
Total	660	100·0	777	100·0

$\chi^2 = 19\cdot8$; $P < 0\cdot001$

TABLE 53.—DISTRIBUTION OF CASES ACCORDING TO PLEA AND
MAGNITUDE OF CHARGE

	Plea					
	Guilty		Not Guilty		Total	
	No.	%	No.	%	No.	%
Homicide	28	100·0	0	0·0	28	100·0
Robbery (3 or more bills of indictment) ..	31	58·5	22	41·5	53	100·0
Robbery (1–2 bills of indictment)	24	29·3	58	70·7	82	100·0
Drugs	59	63·4	34	36·6	93	100·0
Burglary (1–2 bills of indictment)	115	48·3	123	51·7	238	100·0
Burglary (3 or more bills of indictment) ..	54	76·1	17	23·9	71	100·0
Larceny (3 or more bills of indictment) ..	34	48·6	36	51·4	70	100·0
Larceny (1–2 bills of indictment)	114	47·7	125	52·3	239	100·0
Misdemeanours	185	36·8	318	63·2	503	100·0

TABLE 54.—RELATION OF TYPE OF PLEA TO SEVERITY OF SENTENCE WITH OFFENCE CONTROLLED

Sentence	Guilty		Not Guilty	
	No.	%	No.	%
A. Crimes against the person (excluding homicide)				
Prison: 12 mths. and up	8	44·4	19	45·2
Prison: 3–11½ mths. ...	5	27·8	12	28·6
Non-imprisonment ..	5	27·8	11	26·2
Total	18	100·0	42	100·0
$\chi^2 = 0.0$; P = 1				
B. Robbery				
(1) 1–2 bills of indictment				
Prison: 12 mths. and up	8	33·3	19	32·8
Prison: 3–11½ mths. ..	11	45·8	22	37·9
Non-imprisonment ..	5	20·8	17	29·3
Total	24	100·0	58	100·0
$\chi^2 = 0.7$; $0.95 > P > 0.90$				
(2) 3 or more bills of indictment				
Prison: 12 mths. and up	20	64·5	14	63·6
Prison: 3–11½ mths. ..	9	29·0	2	9·1
Non-imprisonment ..	2	6·4	6	27·3
Total	31	100·0	22	100·0
$\chi^2 = 6.4$; $0.50 > P > 0.02$				
C. Narcotics violations				
(1) 1 bill of indictment				
Prison: 12 mths. and up	16	37·2	3	16·7
Prison: 3–11½ mths. ..	10	23·3	10	55·6
Non-imprisonment ..	17	39·5	5	27·7
Total	43	100·0	18	100·0
$\chi^2 = 6.1$; $0.05 > P > 0.02$				
(2) 2 or more bills of indictment				
Prison: 12 mths. and up	8	50·0	10	62·5
Prison: 3–11½ mths. ..	3	18·8	5	31·3
Non-imprisonment ..	5	27·8	1	6·2
Total	16	100·0	16	100·0
$\chi^2 = 0.4$; $0.70 > P > 0.50$				

TABLE 54 (*continued*)

Sentence	Guilty		Not Guilty	
	No.	%	No.	%
D. *Burglary*				
(1) 1–2 bills of indictment				
Prison: 12 mths. and up	20	17·4	22	17·9
Prison: 3–11½ mths. ..	52	45·2	59	48·0
Non-imprisonment ..	43	37·4	42	34·1
Total ..	115	100·0	123	100·0

$\chi^2 = 0\cdot1; 0\cdot95 > P > 0\cdot90$

(2) 3 or more bills of indictment				
Prison: 12 mths. and up	39	72·2	9	53·0
Prison: 3–11½ mths. ..	7	13·0	4	23·5
Non-imprisonment ..	8	14·8	4	23·5
Total ..	54	100·0	17	100·0

$\chi^2 = 2\cdot2; 0\cdot20 > P > 0\cdot10$

E. *Larceny*				
(1) 1–2 bills of indictment				
Prison: 12 mths. and up	15	13·2	25	20·0
Prison: 3–11½ mths. ..	39	34·2	59	47·2
Non-imprisonment ..	60	52·6	41	32·8
Total ..	114	100·0	125	100·0

$\chi^2 = 9\cdot9; P < 0\cdot01$

(2) 3 or more bills of indictment				
Prison: 12 mths. and up	14	41·2	6	16·7
Prison: 3–11½ mths. ..	8	23·5	9	25·0
Non-imprisonment ..	12	35·3	21	58·3
Total ..	34	100·0	36	100·0

$\chi^2 = 5\cdot5; 0\cdot10 > P > 0\cdot05$

F. *Misdemeanours*				
Prison: 12 mths. and up	26	14·0	26	8·2
Prison: 3–11½ mths. ..	44	23·8	96	30·2
Non-imprisonment ..	115	62·2	196	61·0
Total ..	185	100·0	318	100·0

$\chi^2 = 5\cdot5; 0\cdot10 > P > 0\cdot05$

WORKS CITED

Books

Advisory Council of Judges of the National Probation and Parole Association, *Guides for Sentencing*, New York: Carnegie Press, Inc., 1957.

Alexander, Franz, and Staub, Hugo, *The Criminal, the Judge, and the Public*, rev. ed., Glencoe, Illinois: The Free Press, 1956.

Allport, Gordon W., *The Nature of Prejudice*, Cambridge, Massachusetts: Addison Wesley Publishing Co., 1954.

Barnes, Harry Elmer, and Teeters, Negley K., *New Horizons in Criminology*, 2nd ed., New York: Prentice-Hall, Inc., 1951.

Bentham, Jeremy, *The Theory of Legislation*, ed. C. R. Ogden, New York: Harcourt, Brace and Co., 1931.

Caldwell, Robert G., *Criminology*, New York: The Ronald Press Co., 1956.

Cavan, Ruth S., *Criminology*, New York: Thos. Y. Crowell Co., 1955.

Cohen, Morris R., *Reason and Law*, Glencoe, Illinois: The Free Press, 1950.

Elliot, Mabel A., *Crime in Modern Society*, New York: Harper & Bros., 1952.

Hall, Jerome, *Theft, Law, and Society*, 2nd ed., Indianapolis: The Bobbs-Merrill Co., 1952.

Martin, Roscoe, *The Defendant and Criminal Justice*, University of Texas Bulletin No. 3437: Bureau of Research in the Social Sciences, Study No. 9; 1 October, 1934.

O'Regan, Daniel T., and Schlosser, Frank G., *The Criminal Laws of New Jersey*, Vol. 2, New York: Baker, Voorhis and Co., Inc., 1942.

Pollak, Otto, *The Criminality of Women*, Philadelphia: University of Pennsylvania Press, 1950.

Purdon's Pennsylvania Statutes Annotated, Title 18: *Crimes and Offenses*, Title 19: *Criminal Procedure*, Philadelphia: George T. Bisel Co., 1930 (revised to 1952).

Reimel, Theodore L., *Pennsylvania Criminal Law Digest*, Philadelphia: George T. Bisel Co., 1944.

Siegel, Sidney, *Non-parametric Statistics for the Behavioral Sciences*, New York: McGraw-Hill Book Co., Inc., 1956.

Sutherland, Edwin H., and Cressey, Donald E., *Principles of Criminology*, 5th ed., Chicago: J. B. Lippincott Co., 1955.

Warner, Sam Bass, and Cabot, Henry B., *Judges and Law Reform*, Cambridge: Harvard University Press, 1936.

Weihofen, Henry, *The Urge to Punish*, New York: Farrar, Straus and Cudahy, 1956.

Wood, Arthur E., and Waite, John B., *Crime and its Treatment*, New York: American Book Co., 1941.

Articles

Campbell, William J., "Developing Systematic Sentencing Procedures," *Federal Probation*, XVIII (September 1954).

Everson, George, "The Human Element in Justice," *Journal of the American Institute of Criminal Law and Criminology*, X (May 1919).

Frankel, Emil, "The Offender and the Court: A Statistical Analysis of the Sentencing of Delinquents," *Journal of Criminal Law and Criminology*, XXXI (November–December 1940).

Gaudet, Frederick J., Harris, G. S., and St. John, C. W., "Individual Differences in the Sentencing Tendencies of Judges," *Journal of Criminal Law and Criminology*, XXIII (January–February 1933).

Gaudet, Frederick J., Harris, G. S., and St. John, C. W., "Individual Differences in Penitentiary Sentences Given by Different Judges," *Journal of Applied Psychology*, VIII (October 1934).

Gaudet, Frederick J., "Individual Differences in the Sentencing Tendencies of Judges," *Archives of Psychology*, XXII (June 1938).

Gaudet, Frederick J., "The Differences between Judges in the Granting of Sentences of Probation," *Temple Law Quarterly*, XIX (April 1946).

Gaudet, Frederick J., "The Sentencing Behavior of the Judge," *Encyclopedia of Criminology*, eds. V. C. Branham and S. B. Kutash, New York: Philosophical Library, 1949.

Holtzoff, Alexander, "The Judicial Process as Applied to Sentencing in Criminal Cases," *Federal Probation*, XIII (June 1950).

Lane, Harold E., "Illogical Variations in Sentences of Felons Committed to Massachusetts State Prison," *Journal of Criminal Law and Criminology*, XXXII (July–August 1941).

Laub, Burton R., "Sentencing and Release in Pennsylvania — A New Approach," *Temple Law Quarterly*, XXVII (Spring 1954).

Lemert, Edwin M., and Rosberg, Judy, "The Administration of Justice to Minority Groups in Los Angeles County," *University of California Publications in Culture and Society*, Vol. 11, No. 1 (1948).

Levin, Theodore, "Sentencing the Criminal Offender," *Federal Probation*, XIII (March 1949).

McGuire, Matthew F., and Holtzoff, Alexander, "The Problem of Sentencing in the Criminal Law," *Boston University Law Review*, CDXIII (1940).

Ploscowe, Morris, "The Court and the Correctional System," *Contemporary Correction*, ed. Paul Tappan, New York: McGraw-Hill Book Co., Inc. (1951).

Schroeder, Theodore, "The Psychologic Study of Judicial Opinions," *California Law Review*, VI (January 1918).

Sellin, Thorsten, "The Negro Criminal: A Statistical Note," *Annals of the American Academy of Political and Social Science*, CXL (November 1928).

Sellin, Thorsten, "Race Prejudice in the Administration of Justice," *American Journal of Sociology*, XLI (September 1935).

Bibliographies

Institute of Judicial Administration, *Disparity in Sentencing of Convicted Offenders*, New York: April 1954.

INDEX